the guide

to picking up girls

the guide

to picking up girls

GABE FISCHBARG

A PLUME BOOK

PLUME
Published by the Penguin Group
Penguin Putnam Inc., 375 Hudson Street, New York, New York 10014, U.S.A.
Penguin Books Ltd, 80 Strand, London WC2R 0RL, England
Penguin Books Australia Ltd, 250 Camberwell Road, Camberwell, Victoria 3124,
Australia
Penguin Books Canada Ltd, 10 Alcorn Avenue, Toronto, Ontario, Canada M4V 3B2
Penguin Books (N.Z.) Ltd, 182–190 Wairau Road, Auckland 10, New Zealand

Penguin Books Ltd, Registered Offices: Harmondsworth, Middlesex, England

Published by Plume, a member of Penguin Putnam Inc. Originally published by First
Choice Press.

First Plume Printing, October 2002
10 9 8 7 6 5 4 3

 REGISTERED TRADEMARK—MARCA REGISTRADA

LIBRARY OF CONGRESS CATALOGING-IN-PUBLICATION DATA

Fischbarg, Gabe.
    The guide to picking up girls / Gabe Fischbarg.
      p. cm.
    ISBN 0-452-28357-4
    1. Dating (Social customs). 2. Man-woman relationships. 3. Interpersonal commu-
nication. 4. Single men—Psychology. 5. Single men—Life skills guides. I. Title.
HQ801 .F56 2002
646.7'7—dc21

                                                          2002074809

Printed in the United States of America
Set in Futura Book
Designed by Leonard Telesca

Women represent the triumph of matter over mind, just as men represent the triumph of mind over morals.

—Oscar Wilde

Boy meets girl, so what?

—Bertolt Brecht

What do women want?

—Sigmund Freud

Contents

Introduction

Beautiful girl in the corner. You are nervous. You are afraid. How do you approach her? What should you say first? Would you be able to handle a rejection?

Some of the hardest things in life: going to a job interview, starting a new job, taking a test, speaking in front of an audience, moving to a new city and *laying rap on chicks.*

How do you start a rap? How do you avoid lame pick-up lines? How do you overcome a fear of rejection? When do you make your move? *What do you say?* These and other questions will be answered as we help you build a master rap!

You Have The Guide in Your Hands

We call this book The Guide. In your hands is the essential guide to picking up girls.

It contains the truth about the way guys and girls really talk and act. The Guide pulls no punches and holds nothing back. It includes all the true things that people think and know but are afraid to say out loud.

For example, The Guide understands, like you do, that there are many different types of girls you will meet in life. There are pretty girls and there are ugly girls. There are girls who are bitches and there are girls who are not. There are sluts and whores and nice girls too. The Guide will help you to understand all of them and explain how you should deal with them when you are picking them up.

The Guide Is Not a Dating Book, It Is for Picking Up Girls

You may read The Guide and then hit it off with someone on your first night out. Put this book away and date the girl.

The Guide is not a dating book. The Guide can help you on a date, but it was not written for that purpose. Although many of the principles discussed here can carry over into a date (e.g., your attitude or dialogue topics), The Guide's true aim is to get you on that date. Indeed, what you say on a date can be quite different from what you say when picking up a girl. The Guide is for picking up girls at a party, a club, a bar, a wedding, etc. The Guide was not written to tell you exactly what to say on a first, second, third or fourth date. This is purely a manual on how to pick up a girl and get her phone number.

Sometimes, if you are aggressive enough in following The Guide and your rap is clicking, you may get more than just the phone number on the same night you meet a girl. There may be simple, innocent fooling around—making out with the girl at the place where you met her (or on the sidewalk outside that place). Serious fooling around involves bringing the girl back to your place (or her place) the same night you meet her. Each is possible, but your main goal should just be the phone number. Don't expect that you will experience a "*Penthouse* Forum" story every other month. In fact, don't expect that such an experience will ever happen. Just be happy with getting the phone number. Once you secure the phone number and you think pushing it further won't hurt you in the future, then you can try for more. If alcohol is involved, you have a much better chance: The girl subconsciously knows she can blame the alcohol the next day if she feels she went too far with you. Remember, however, that alcohol shouldn't be used to take advantage of the girl. The alcohol is just a bonus that will make the girl friendlier.

The Guide will also show you that many things you thought were true are merely myths. For example, one myth is that if a girl fools around with you on the same night you meet her, she is not girlfriend material. In fact, just the opposite is true. That girl is probably not uptight about sex and is self-assured and confident enough not to go nutty after fooling around with a boy. When you do go out with her on your first real date, do not try to fool around with her. This will show her that you respect her and that you don't just want to go out with her because she's easy—even if that is the real reason. More on this later.

If The Guide serves its purpose and you start dating one girl exclusively, you can then give the book to some other guy. Make sure to get it back if you break up with the girl.

If you've been out of commission from hitting on girls because you have had a girlfriend for a while, most likely you will be out of practice with your rap. You will need to reread The Guide or at least the parts you have forgotten. Soon enough you will be back in shape.

You will be at your lowest confidence level if a girl you really like won't go out with you or breaks up with you (i.e., "I will never meet anyone else ever again"). The Guide will give you the confidence to jump on another horse in no time. Don't get discouraged if you are rusty for a few weeks or months. A good rap takes time. A great invincible, bulletproof rap won't come immediately. It requires practice, timing, a little confidence and, of course, a girl to talk to.

Some of the stuff in The Guide is commonsense stuff that you might already know. Some of the stuff you might have had in the back of your mind but never thought out completely. The Guide now brings it all together.

This manual was written for picking up girls both in social situations, like a party or a wedding, and in public settings, like a supermarket or the post office. However, be aware that laying rap in a public setting has a lower percentage of success than in a social situation.

Don't let your expectations get too far ahead of you. You will not get a girl's phone number every night that you go out. That is the law of averages. Sometimes you can't beat the odds, but The Guide will help you maximize the opportunities that exist in your favor.

A main feature of The Guide is a list of questions and topics for laying a relaxed and confident rap that can be tailored to your specific needs. But first you must get a grip on some myths, ground rules and the background situations involved in picking up girls.

the guide

to picking up girls

chapter

1

Getting Prepared for Laying Rap

A *Girl* Is What You Want

Girl is the word to be used here and always. *Chick* can sometimes be used. No political correctness is necessary in The Guide. A girl is whom you want to go out with. You don't want a *woman*. A woman is your mother and your grandmother. A nice, attractive girl is what you want. Nothing wrong with calling a girl a girl.

A *Rap* Is What You Say When Talking to a Girl

Teaching you to lay a good rap on a girl is the goal of The Guide. Many people think their rap is not really them, but instead is just an adopted persona, a fake attitude to put on when trying to pick up a girl. That is only partially true. The best rap is one that matches your own personality. A fake attitude or rap is hard to pull off and can come off as obviously fake. Improving your own attitude, outlook on life and personality is the first step to giving yourself a master rap.

Creating, developing and refining the master rap can take time. Improving your rap and honing your rap skills should be a long-term project. A master rap will not fall from the sky; it requires practice and time. The Guide will help you get that master rap all guys are seeking.

Being Nervous Is Not an Option

Remember this phrase: "Look hungry, go hungry." Don't act desperate. Rent the movie *Swingers* and pay close attention to the Trent character's speech about how the guy is the big bear with claws and the girl is just a little bunny you can rip apart with your superb rap. The same way you can sense if a girl is desperate, a girl can easily sense if you are acting too anxious. A girl can smell a desperate guy a mile away. Put yourself in her place: Do you want to date some nervous, shifty guy or a guy with confidence, exuding a healthy feeling of self-worth?

Being nervous is not an option. The Guide will help you lose any nervousness you may have. If you are nervous, see the section on alcohol on page 76 of The Guide.

Once you have sufficient confidence, it doesn't really matter so much what you say because you will exude a free and easy attitude. You will be fearless, bulletproof and totally aware of the situation around you. You will be able to say anything you want without any hesitation. In the old days, before you read The Guide, you might have been nervous, clueless and afraid of every little thing you said. You might have lost your rap and wallowed in self-pity and despair. After you read The Guide, you will understand how to conquer your fears and nerves.

Poised, confident, relaxed, happy, smooth, charming, laid-back, funny and *warm;* these adjectives should all apply to you and your rap. When you get to your party destination on your night out, there is no reason why you can't act like you actually own the place. Have you ever seen the owner at his bar or the host at his own party? They are on top of the world and as happy as can be. They have the right attitude for laying rap on girls.

Remember that preparation is the natural enemy of nervousness. The Guide will prepare you for anything and everything.

Forget Your Ancient History of Bad Experiences

Traumatized in high school? You and everybody else. Forget all the high school, college or postcollege rejections and girls who ignored you. It doesn't matter. Girls can be mean and full of anger. Forget them. The time for anger is over. It's time to party and have fun.

You Don't Have to "Just Be Yourself"

One myth we often hear about picking up girls is that you should "just be yourself." Wrong. "Being yourself" means nothing because you are constantly changing. You are a different person at twenty than you are at twenty-five, and, likewise, you are different at thirty than you are at thirty-five, etc.

You can always change the way you think and act. You can mold your rap to work best for you. Forget about "just being yourself." You are whatever person you want to create.

A similar myth is that "people never change." People can, and do, change a lot. You can always change the way you think, the way you act and the way you rap with girls. Your rap is undergoing constant change as you refine and perfect it.

It is true that some people never change. They either don't want to or need to, or they are afraid to. It is obvious that a person's failure to change can cause the end of a friendship, a romantic relationship or a marriage. The failure to change can also destroy families, companies and entire countries. In comparison, the ability to adapt causes technological advances, improved health care, growing economies and long-lasting personal relationships.

Developing a Philosophy of
Life and Quieting the Voices in Your Head

Mastering the skill of picking up girls requires that you develop a philosophy of life. You cannot go through life aimlessly and without understanding who you are. That lack of focus will be picked up on by the girls you talk to and will turn them off. Girls want someone who is centered, directed and has an attitude.

When describing a guy, a girl will sometimes say, "Oh, he's not manly enough" or "He's still just a boy." What she means is that the guy has no focus, nothing for them to get a handle on. You don't necessarily need to grow up or be a serious adult immediately, you just need to get a little edge, some attitude and some confidence. Remember that you don't need to be a jerk or be mean to have an attitude. Just be focused, happy and confident. You can adjust and adapt your attitude depending on the girl you talk to.

Much of life is dealing with what your conscience tells you; learning how to listen, *and when not to listen*, to those voices in your head telling you what you should and shouldn't do. This ability comes from our biological instincts, which sometimes must be controlled.

As a starting point, all laws in existence today are the result of man's instincts or internal drive, which must be reigned in and controlled. In the caveman days, man would act on his instincts without much control. He took what he wanted. He killed when he wanted. He grabbed a woman he thought desirable without worrying about any consequences.

Over time, as man allegedly evolved, laws were created. Man could no longer take the property of another just because he was stronger than the other man. Man could no longer beat someone up that he didn't like just because he felt like it. If he tried these things in modern society, he might go to prison.

Except for the few who practice criminal behavior for a living, men have had their basest instincts suppressed and controlled by society. Even some criminals follow most of society's rules and decide to break only one rule at a time.

Unfortunately, we grow up learning 10,000 different rules, which are in conflict with our natural instincts. These instincts have been inhibited and molded by various outside influences. People (parents, religious figures, teachers, friends, relatives, etc.) are constantly telling us to be careful of this and to watch out for that. We are constantly being told what is good behavior and what is bad behavior.

Suddenly, we have all these voices in our heads telling us what to do, what not to do, what we are allowed to say and what we are not allowed to say. These voices are helpful in some situations, such as getting along with friends and family and doing well at work or school. But in the area of picking up girls, the voices in your head can be your enemy. They tell you to avoid risks and be careful, and they can inspire fear, nervousness and shyness. While those voices can help you survive a climb up a mountain or driving in traffic, they should not be listened to when picking up girls. You have to learn to listen to the voices that will help you, and ignore the ones that won't.

The problem is that society has also infected our conscience regarding picking up girls. In everyday life, we are taught to be conservative, careful and safe. The voices in your head reflect the sum of all you have learned from society. But the rules and laws of society have nothing to do with picking up girls, so the voices in your head do not apply. They can stifle your natural instincts to be aggressive, bold and confident. You must control the voices in your head. You must shut them up and quiet them down. This will help you overcome any unnecessary inhibitions. Picking up girls is not a part of life that requires you to be very careful. When you pick up girls, you are now back in the caveman days, beyond the rigid and inflexible rules of society.

Alcohol, your good friend and magic elixir, is particularly helpful in showing you the way. Alcohol removes our unnecessary inhibitions. That is why it remains a legal drug. More on this later.

Picking up girls gives you a chance to be creative, aggressive and confident. Anything can happen when you start laying a rap, and you can take chances. The risks are not great and there is nothing to fear.

Remember: Fortune favors the bold. Do not hold anything back. Laying rap and perfecting it are fun, exciting and challenging activities. Developing a good rap should be one of your life's goals, outside of your other, more boring, daily pursuits.

Don't Be Jealous of Other Guys

Jealousy is one of the seven deadly sins for a very good reason. It is innately human and sometimes impossible to avoid, but it should be controlled and suppressed as much as possible.

Don't be jealous of guys you think are better looking than you. Don't be jealous of guys you think have a better rap than you do. They have their own problems and insecurities, and your rap can be just as good as theirs with a little practice and with The Guide to help you. As Shakespeare noted, jealousy is the "green-eyed monster" that can consume and destroy people. If anything, instead of being jealous of someone, you should try to learn from that person as much as possible. Copy that person's style, their attitude and even their rap. If it works for them, it should work for you.

This positive attitude should carry over when you are laying rap on a girl. There is nothing less attractive than jealousy or anger. Don't let a girl think you have a serious jealous streak or are capable of intense anger. Telling a girl about a funny pet peeve is okay.

It is okay to tell a story about someone that annoyed you recently, like a dentist who left a needle in your jaw while he left the room, or a flight attendant who spilled coffee on you. Acting annoyed at something silly like that is all right. But you cannot cross the line and act like you intensely hate the person you are talking about. There is a fine line between being annoyed at someone and hating him or her, and acting seriously hateful or jealous of anyone must be avoided.

There is no reason to be jealous of anyone. Ever. Remember, even the good-looking jocks in high school and college have major insecurities and hang-ups. Many of them did poorly in school academically. They know that everyone thinks they are stupid.

How would you like to be a dumb good-looking guy if your whole life everyone knew you were stupid and only talked to you for phony reasons? Or if you were a dumb jock who was always afraid that if you hurt your knee, no one would be your friend anymore? You wouldn't like it

They are not your enemy. You have no enemies except yourself.

There is nothing to worry about. Soon, you too will have the master rap.

The Mission

You are on a mission.

Your mission is to impose your will on a girl. You are going to convince the girl that you are the guy she should want. She will believe that you are what she is looking for.

She can't do better than you. You have it all, including a happy outlook on life and a superior and confident demeanor.

There is no reason that you should be nervous before you approach a girl. There is no reason any girl should make you nervous. You are there to choose and take the girl you want. The girl is not picking you, you are picking the girl. You are taking the girl into your world. You are taking what you want.

You are letting her know that you bring more to the table than she does. Just because her body is female does not give her any advantage over you. You have the advantage over her because you have the power to be fun, entertaining and confident. She may also be fun, entertaining and confident, but you are completing the puzzle for her. She needs *you* to be fun, entertaining and confident. That is something she wants. That is something all girls want.

You are there to set her straight. Don't let her complain about her worries in the world. Your job is to convince her how great the world is, how happy she should be and how to get that way. So if she says something down and negative, you should not let her get away with it. Make her realize things are not so bad and that she should be happy. Show her how happy and confident you are, and you will win her over. Pretty soon, your warmth and confidence will rub off and she will want to talk to you.

This is not to say that your happiness should be phony.

You should sincerely believe that life is mostly fun even if you might be dealing with your own problems. This night, with some drinks in you, there are no worries. It is time for fun.

The beginning part of your rap should not focus on trying to convince the girl right away that she has to go on a date with you. It is more about making the girl feel comfortable. Get her into a relaxed, fun state, not a state where she is worried about you as a possible sexual predator. Girls admire a guy who is "charming," meaning smooth, relaxed, comfortable, cool, calm and collected. But it does not mean quiet and mysterious. You still have to draw out the girl and entertain her a little.

Once you have broken down any barriers the girl has put up, you can move on to the aggressive flirting. A good rap is about knowing how to break down these barriers. Girls can come in many moods: nervous, shy, distracted about getting over a boyfriend, distracted about trying to dump a boyfriend, wary of guys being too aggressive, wary of guys trying phony pick-up lines on her, snooty, aloof, a little cranky, a little tired, etc. A good rap will break down any of those "barriers" and change the girl's attitude.

Of course, the best girl is the one who is already in a good, flirty mood. It makes your job a lot easier. But even if she is distracted or a little cranky, if her switch is just a little bit "on," meaning she is even slightly interested, she will give you a chance to lay rap.

Do not put yourself down in any way. Do not ever disclose that a girl ever dumped you. No girl has ever dumped you. You dumped all of them.

Do not talk about specific girls you have dated. Do not talk about ex-girlfriends. Your dating history must be kept to yourself. It is understood that you can get a date anytime you want.

If you can't hear something she said, tell her. Don't try to skip over it and ignore it. You must hear everything she says to get in the groove and feel the situation. The girl will think you are cool if you tell her you can't hear her. It will show her that you pay attention to what she says.

It is often so loud in a club that you can't hear the girl. Try to get her to go to an area where you can hear each other better. The bar is usually more quiet. Clubs don't put speakers near bartenders so they can hear what drinks a customer wants.

chapter

2

Overcoming the Fear
of Rejection

Figuring Out Which Girl Has Her Switch On
and Which Girl Has Her Switch Off

The most common difficulty most guys initially have is a
fear of rejection. After a guy talks to three different girls
and none are interested in him, he may give up, demoralized and hurt. He should not worry or become angry. He
only lacks some understanding of the situation.

Girls out at night come in only two forms: those with
their switches "on" and those with their switches "off."

As you know, a girl will go out in many different
groups. Sometimes a girl will go out with only one other
girl, sometimes with a few other girls, sometimes with
many other girls. Sometimes they will be in a group of
girls and guys together.

A girl with her switch "off" is not looking to meet a new guy. If a girl has her switch off, it could be because:

- she has a boyfriend
- she is engaged
- she is married (look for a ring and ask her if she is married, because a ring might not be a wedding ring)
- she is interested in only one guy in particular at that time
- she has just broken up with a guy and hates men for now
- she is a lesbian (for real)
- she has personal family problems she is dealing with
- she is on a girls' night out (more on that later)
- she can only talk to her girlfriends that night (e.g., a reunion, a birthday party)
- she is out with people from work
- she is too drunk and is ready to go home

Believe it or not, some girls are out just for the sake of being out. They didn't want to sit at home alone that night. Even if a girl has a boyfriend, she can't necessarily go out with him every night of the week. The boyfriend might be busy, in which case the girl will still want to go out and spend time with her girlfriends.

A girl might be angry at the world and not want to talk to anyone, but that won't stop her from going out just for the sake of going. That way, if anyone asks her what she did that weekend, she can say that she went out and she won't have to say that she did nothing and stayed home watching TV. Going out and blowing guys off all night is better than staying home and doing nothing, right?

A girl out with people from work may be reluctant to flirt with a strange guy at a party or a club. She may not want her coworkers to think she is slutty. Rumors may start at work, and she will be asked a hundred questions the next day about "what happened with that guy?"

The same thing is true about a group of girls on a girls' night out. She can't necessarily peel away from the rest of her group and talk to you. She may be worried that her friends will get offended if she ditches them to talk to you, or that they will be jealous of her or think she's easy.

One thing to do is to say this out in the open to her: "Can you talk to me with people from your work around?" "Can you talk to me even on your girls' night out, or will your friends get mad at you?"

Naturally, if a girl does not have her switch off, then she has her switch on. This means she is looking for a boyfriend and will give practically any guy a chance to talk to her.

It is important to remember that having a boyfriend usually means everything to a girl. Many girls are so insecure that their entire self-worth is wrapped up in whether or not they have a boyfriend. A girl may be inclined to offend her best girlfriend if it means she will get a boyfriend. Indeed, you will hear many girls complain about a girlfriend who disappears once she has a boyfriend, only to reappear if the new boyfriend doesn't work out.

In the extreme view, as the humorist Antoine de Rivarol remarked, "Friendship among women is only a suspension of hostilities." H. L. Mencken noted that "When women kiss, it always reminds one of prize fighters shaking hands."

Do not let girls you do not know well find out that you know about these things. Confronting girls about their worst character traits is not a good idea. It is good enough that you know the truth.

Once a girl has her switch on, all you have to do is lay a little rap on her. She will usually give you her full attention.

Maybe you don't realize how easy laying a good rap really is. The reason for that is that most guys have terrible raps. Most guys don't know how to talk to girls in the right way. Most guys have no hobbies or interests that girls like. All most guys know are sports, business, drinking, and that's it. Most guys that girls meet at night act too drunk and too obnoxious. Since you won't act that way, and since you will know how to talk to a girl correctly, you will have a big advantage.

Again, a girl with her switch on is what you are constantly looking for. Unfortunately, there is no way to tell which girls have their switches on and which have them off until you actually talk to them. Many people make the mistake of assuming a girl has her switch off without actually talking to the girl. Because a girl is talking intently to her girlfriend, you might mistakenly assume that her switch is off. If the girl never looks around past the girlfriend, then this may be true. But she may be stuck in a conversation only because her girlfriend wants desperately to talk to her about something she thinks is important. The girlfriend, rather than the girl you like, could have her switch off. Thus, you don't need to make any hard assumptions as to which girl has her switch off. Stay flexible and expect a girl who looks like she has it off to actually have it on. The opposite can also be true. A girl might seem so flirtatious and outgoing that her switch must certainly be on. Suddenly, out of the blue, she says, "Oh, I can't, I have a boyfriend."

The key is to figure out as soon as possible whether the switch is on or off. If the girl has her switch off, find out fast and move on. *You have not been rejected.* Do not feel rejected, do not feel demoralized, do not despair. You are ice, bulletproof, made of steel. Her switch was not on. *She has a boyfriend. It was not you.*

At a strictly "singles" event, there won't be any girls with their switches off. At singles events, the girls are usually very receptive. However, competition for the very pretty girls is sometimes fierce at these events. Every guy there thinks they have a good shot at getting a date and will act very aggressively. That's why following The Guide will give you the advantage.

Learn the Girl

Once you start your rap, get the feel of the situation. Figure out where the girl is coming from.

The first rule when giving a speech is learning about your audience ahead of time. The same is true when you are laying rap. One of your first tasks when you start talking to the girl is to figure out what the girl is looking for in a guy. Try to pick up on her hints. If she's talking about traveling, don't talk about sports. If she's talking about sports, don't talk about traveling.

Remember that the girl is often trying to figure you out while you are trying to figure her out. Act like a mirror and just give her what she wants. Make her think you are listening to her every word, even though you might be thinking about what she looks like naked. Make her feel like she is the only girl in the world. Do not look around while you are talking to her.

Just as important: Do not talk about other girls at all. Do not talk about ex-girlfriends or other dates you have had. Do not describe how a certain girl did not like you. Do not talk about a one-night stand you had two years ago. Do not talk about how a girl once broke your heart or about how you broke a girl's heart.

If you are forced to talk about other girls you have dated, as far as the girl you are talking to knows, all girls have liked you and no girl has ever broken up with you. You have broken up with all the girls you have dated. A girl has never hurt you, and you have never had a problem with girls.

You don't need to stare at her nonstop. You should try to act a little cool and disinterested, but don't look away at a hot girl if one walks by. Try to become more animated, excited and interested as the rap goes on. Do not start the rap by acting immediately like you are head-over-heels, madly in love with the girl.

You Don't Need to Act Like a Jerk When Laying Rap

Some people think you must act like a jerk to get a girl. Many guys adopt the dickhead, obnoxious, asshole rap when talking to a girl. The asshole rap will work sometimes, so many people think that is a way to go.

Everyone knows that girls don't like the nice guy, right? We've all heard it. Nice guys finish last. This is only partially true. In truth, girls don't like guys who are weak. Girls like guys who are tough and have confidence. You can be nice to the girl without acting weak. You must show the girl that you are in command. That is why you can't act nervous. The key to a good rap is showing interest in the girl without any air of desperation, weakness or insecurity. Show the girl that you are supremely balanced: tough, confident and nice all at the same time.

Boxers often talk about imposing their will on an opponent in order to defeat him. Brute strength will not necessarily win the day in the first round. Rather, a smooth and skilled wearing down of the opponent will eventually cause the victory. That is why Roberto Duran said *"No más"* to Sugar Ray Leonard in the middle of the fight. His will had been broken. Similarly, as you get into your rap, you can start to impose your will on the girl. You can't use brutish, obnoxious dialogue. Rather, imposing your will on the girl is a subtle exercise in getting the girl to realize that you are happy, successful, always in complete control and without fear of any hazards in life.

Again, if you look hungry, you will go hungry. But if you look full, you will become more full. And that's a good thing.

Always Look to Be Trading Up

It's good to go out and lay rap on girls even if you are casually dating a girl or have a date coming up. It helps your confidence level if you know you already have a date with another girl in the near future. This will keep your options open until you actually start going out with one girl exclusively. It is always easier to talk to a potential "backup" than the "first string" girl. You will feel that your rap is relaxed and natural with the potential backup girl. You have nothing to lose, so your effort will be without pressure. This is an important way to refine and practice your rap. Sometimes the backup will even make it into the starting lineup if it doesn't work out with the first girl.

It may be difficult, but it is better not to break up with

a girl until you have a new girl set up. It may be cruel to the girl you want to break up with, but start laying rap on new girls when you realize you want to start phasing out your current girlfriend. Your rap will naturally be better and more relaxed. You probably don't realize how much having a girlfriend subconsciously and automatically helps your rap with other girls.

Find Out the Girl's Name Quickly and Use It During the Rap

After the initial ice-breaking conversation with a girl, find out her name as soon as possible and *don't forget it*. Many people say they are not good with names. You should not be one of those people.

A common difficulty arises when you are introduced to a girl and several of her friends at the same time. Can you remember the girl's name *and* the names of her three friends? It's not easy, especially with some vodka in your bloodstream.

But there are many simple tricks for remembering a person's name after they tell it to you. The human brain can remember a piece of information easier if that piece of information is linked together with something else in the mind.

One way is to associate the person with an animal immediately as they tell you their name. If she looks like a cat and her name is Diane, in your head she is "Diane the Cat." If she looks mousy and her name is Cathy, in your head she is "Cathy the Mouse."

Another method is to rhyme the name you hear with something else immediately. The more unusual or sexual the rhyme, the better.

Girl's name: Amy
Rhyme: "Lay Me, Amy"

Girl's name: Jessica
Rhyme: "Messy Jesse"

Girl's name: Monica
Rhyme: "Monica the Harmonica"

Girl's name: Judy
Rhyme:"Prudy Judy"

Yet another method is to link the girl's name with another word with the same first letter (also known as an alliteration or a pneumonic). This method is fairly easy: Pretty Paula, Friendly Frances, Luscious Liz and Lovely Linda.

You will score huge points if you can remember not only the girl's name but also the names of her girlfriends. Since every little bit will help you score with a girl, you should make the effort to remember her friends' names.

Now that you know the girl's name, it is important to say it a few times while you are talking to her. People like to hear their own names. Hearing your own name said to you makes you feel good on a subconscious level. Psychiatrists say it reminds you of your childhood when your parents were calling out to you in a loving manner.

However, pick and choose carefully when you say the girl's name during your rap because people don't like to hear it repeated too much. We all know those really annoying people who constantly repeat your name when they are talking to you. Pushy salespeople usually do this because they, too, are taught that people like to hear their names. It is always good to say the person's name right before you say something a little flirtatious or bold: "So, Julie, do you have a boyfriend?" "So, Jennifer, are you listed in the phone book?"

Telling a girl she has a pretty name is okay as long as you don't make a big thing about it. If she has an unusually pretty name (e.g., Cleo, Chloe, Amber, Starr, Storm, Desiree, etc.), she has probably heard from a lot of guys what a beautiful name she has.

Do Not Waste Time with Mean Girls

Anytime you go out, odds are that there are some girls out there who are in a bad mood. If you start rapping with a girl and she puts you down in any way, be careful. If it does not look like she is joking and she is truly mean, do not put up with that shit. Her switch is off. Stop talking to her.

By dissing her, you are recognizing that she is not worth the effort of your rap. Your rap should be preserved for a girl who has her switch on. A girl with her switch off is not worthy of your time, conversation and attention.

Remember that *you do not need to put up with any negativity. You are in control.* You must have the discipline to remove yourself from a bad situation and talk to a girl who is receptive; again, only talk to a girl who has her switch on.

It does not matter if the girl with her switch off has a pretty face. Her switch is off and you cannot talk to her. Look for another pretty girl. If there are no other pretty girls, then you are in the wrong place that night.

Do not become offended if a girl is mean to you. It is not your problem or fault; some people are simply mean individuals. Many people had bad childhoods and haven't resolved their childhood issues. Some people might be dealing with family or work problems. Others can't get past previous bad relationships, etc.

Again, if the girl is acting uninterested and looking around while you are trying to talk to her, stop talking to her. Don't even complete your sentence. Her switch is off. You don't need to even know the reason why it is off. It does not matter why.

If the girl does not ask you any questions about yourself, that is a big tip-off that her switch is off. Usually a girl will want to know the basic facts about you: where you grew up, where you live, where you work, etc. If she doesn't ask you any of these things or doesn't appear interested in them or you during your rap, her switch is off. You don't need to entertain a girl unnecessarily unless you want to practice your rap.

If a girl insults you in an unprovoked matter, do not become angry. Instead, ask her if she's insulting you. If she says yes, ask her why. Tell her you don't understand why she's acting this way, and that if she doesn't want to talk to you, that's fine. Her switch is off. Tell her to have a good night and walk away.

If she's in a group and is acting cliquish, make a joke about it. "Is this your group and you can't leave it to talk to me?" Or, "Oh, are you in a clique and can't leave it to talk to me?" Usually they respond with something like "Oh, I haven't seen these girls in like a year and it's Rachel's birthday." Whatever. No problem. Her switch is off. Tell her you'll be around if she gets free and move on.

No Girl Is Too Pretty for You to Talk To

Many girls complain that guys are intimidated by them and that they have a hard time getting a date because guys are afraid to talk to them and ask them out. Those are usually the pretty girls, and you should not be intimidated by them. They have just as many insecurities as ugly girls, if not more. The key is whether the girl has her switch on, not whether she is so pretty as to be intimidating to men.

A pretty girl is no better than you are, and a good rap will work on her as much as on any other girl who has her switch on. If you look at men objectively, they all pretty much look the same. A few men might be extremely handsome, but most are normal, average and healthy-looking. Thus, you don't need to be devastatingly good-looking to pick up girls. You just need confidence and a decent rap. Accordingly, don't be afraid of a pretty girl. Just go and talk to her and find out if her switch is on or off.

As it happens, many extremely hot girls have their switches off because they are more likely to have boyfriends and tend not to be single for very long. Therefore, if your usually excellent rap is not working on an extremely hot girl, it is not because she is too special to talk to. It is because her switch is off.

Some Girls Won't Talk to Strangers

Many girls won't let you talk to them "cold." They require that somebody they know introduce you to them. To them, you are a stranger. It's stupid but very common. Many girls have to make sure that a guy they date has been preapproved in some way by someone they know. There is nothing you can do. Many insecure girls fear the question, "So, how did you and your boyfriend meet?" They don't want to have to answer, "Oh, we met in a bar." The insecure girl doesn't want her girlfriends to think she got picked up by some random guy in some random place. They need to feel more important by being able to say "Oh, we were introduced by Jill's boyfriend at a party" or "He was one of the guys in the wedding party at Gary and Jennifer's wedding."

Intuitively, the insecure girl's theory makes no sense. If you are at a certain bar, there is no reason that a girl as nice and normal as you can't be there too. The more secure girls will understand this and not be uptight about how they meet their boyfriends.

If you sense that a girl is uptight about how she meets a guy, the best strategy is to start talking to someone who is hanging out with the girl. After a few minutes, ask that person to introduce you to her.

It is always a good idea to do some intelligence and information gathering. For example, if you are at a bar or a club and there is a girl's birthday party going on, talk to the birthday girl and wish her a happy birthday. After talking to her for a few minutes, ask her which of her girlfriends are available. You can ask her to introduce you to her girlfriends, or you can lay rap on your own. At least, since you've already gotten the intelligence, you know which girl in the group has a boyfriend.

Similarly, if you are at a wedding or a party, find out through the groom or the person throwing the party which girl at the event is single and does not have a boyfriend.

Worry About Your Looks

"Girls are only looking for a guy with a good sense of humor." *That is B.S.* and we all know it. As the comedian Gilbert Gottfried has said, "That's why Tom Selleck gets no girls and Shemp in the Three Stooges gets all the girls. Girls will trample over Tom Selleck and rip their clothes apart when they see Shemp across the room."

The next section includes simple workout tips to give you a better body and better looks. Most books or guides about exercise and working out are too general for our purposes. The Guide concentrates only on working on those parts of your body that matter the most to girls. If you are in a hurry and don't have a lot of time to work out, just concentrate on the important areas and forget those that don't help your rap.

Remember that looks do matter, but not as much as you think. A good-looking guy with no rap is worthless. "All looks and no rap" is what the girls will say about him.

As mentioned before, most guys look pretty much alike. Looking at people as being part of a huge bell curve, you'll notice a few people are at the extreme good-looking side, a few are at the extreme ugly side, but most are pretty much in the middle. Guys don't look that much different from one another with their clothes on. That's why having a good rap can be a big help. And the key to a good rap is not so much your looks but *your happiness level*.

One key to a good rap is your happiness quotient. If

you are a happy person, you will have no problem getting girls. It sounds silly, but think about it: A girl who is pretty from a distance but has a nasty attitude once you meet her is suddenly no longer pretty. An average-looking girl with a happy, friendly attitude becomes a very hot girl.

Same thing is true with guys. A regular guy who is happy and fun is always better looking than the super handsome guy who is sour and has no rap. Happy people look better and are more attractive.

We often hear the theory that girls are only looking for a guy with a sense of humor. It is in every "chick" magazine you see. But it is an idea that is only partially true. What's more accurate is that guys should have a happy and fun attitude. Girls aren't looking for a silly comedian cracking jokes every two seconds. Girls want to be with a happy, fun guy who also can be funny every now and then.

But looks are still a factor. Get yourself in the best position you can. Get a nice haircut, some nice clothes. Look clean. Don't be cheap in fixing yourself up. Being penny-wise and pound-foolish will hurt you big. Getting yourself dressed up and looking nice before you go out will naturally build your confidence and your rap.

One myth is that you need a lot of expensive clothes to look good. In reality, you don't need a lot of different outfits. All you need to have is a few nice outfits. You can just rotate them. Even if you see the same girl that you talked to on an earlier night, she won't necessarily remember what you were wearing the first time you met her. To be safe, when you go on repeated dates with the same girl, remember exactly what you wear every time you see her. To be very safe, write it down.

Avoid wearing the same outfit twice as long as possible. Remember, too, that she will have the same fear about repeating her outfits as you do.

Although it is nice to be all pumped up and excited to go out, once you've put on a nice outfit, you don't need to get too cocky. Remember, you still may not succeed immediately if the first girl you meet has her switch off.

You must also be dressed appropriately in comparison to what others are wearing. A downtown club requires dark clothes, while a "happy hour" place, with an after-work crowd, requires a suit. An upscale bar calls for a blazer. At a regular bar, wear a nice button-down shirt. Meanwhile, a dive demands only a T-shirt.

It is always better to be overdressed than underdressed. Very important: Never wear sneakers or a baseball cap out at night.

Having a good job and making good money also helps plenty. But if you don't have a rap, those things won't help you.

Finally, everyone looks good with a suntan. But do not overdo it. You don't want to look older than your age when you reach your thirties, forties or fifties. You really shouldn't get a tan more than three times a year if you want to avoid age lines or sun damage. For a real scare, take a look at women and men who tanned too much when they were young. They look like lizards. In addition, remember to tan and not burn; a burnt, red face will not help your rap.

Working-Out Tips

Working out and giving yourself some attractive muscles automatically adds to your confidence level. Aerobic activity will increase your ability to handle alcohol, since your body will be able to metabolize alcohol better and help you lose your hangover more quickly. This type of exercise will improve your heart's strength and ability to pump blood. There are plenty of fat people who are in excellent aerobic condition (i.e., have strong hearts).

Therefore, you must do aerobic activity that not only increases your heart's strength but also burns fat. Usually the two go hand in hand! But some aerobic activities are better than others in burning fat. The best options are rowing (at least twelve minutes using the right form), running (at least forty minutes required) and roller-blading (at least thirty minutes).

Avoid biking, swimming and the Stairmaster. They are not as efficient in burning calories and increasing your heart's strength.

Also, a regular aerobics class is for girls and gay men. Avoid them.

Spinning classes, boot-camp classes and aero-boxing are okay if other aerobic activities bore you.

The muscles that girls notice first are the chest, neck and arms. If you don't have a lot of time to work out, just do biceps, triceps, back pull-downs, upright rows and chest (bench press). If you have only a little time to work out, forget legs, stomach and shoulders.

Thinning Hair

Some guys lose confidence if their hair is thinning or receding. Avoid comb-overs or messy hair if you are losing your hair. Just get your hair cut short.

Remember that men are taller than women. Most women can't see the top of your head and won't see it for a long time. A girl most likely won't see the top of your head until you are both sitting down or lying down horizontally, at which time it won't matter. As one bald friend likes to rhyme, "If your rap is there, she won't care about your hair." If you have a happy, confident rap, you'll be fine.

Hair loss is a function of the aging process. You can stay younger-looking by constantly doing aerobic activity and drinking a lot of water. Don't ever be thirsty. If you get thirsty, it means your body is already two cups below the amount of water it normally should have.

Use Rogaine or the cheaper generic drug Minoxidil if you want to boost your confidence. No one knows if Minoxidil works. But it is cheap now and can be purchased over the counter at a drugstore.

Multivitamins, antioxidant vitamins and inositol (a type of vitamin B) are also supposed to help slow down the aging process. Getting enough sleep is also key.

You must avoid the sagging, double-chin problem. It is a dead giveaway that you are letting yourself go, and girls can notice it for sure. You must do aerobic exercise at a minimal level to avoid the sagging chin. Just lifting weights (anaerobic exercise) will not help. Only aerobic exercise will cause you to lose fat, increase your heart rate and remove the double chin.

Props and Games

Some guys use props for fun and as part of their rap with girls. Some are okay and some are quite worthless.

A good prop at a party or fund-raiser is a disposable camera or a small regular camera. Don't use a big bulky camera with a fancy lens. That will make you look too much like a stalker type. You can start rapping with girls before or after you take the picture. Don't ask to take a picture, just tell them you are going to do it, then do it. A better thing to do is to give the camera to other people and have them take a picture of you and the girl or girls.

Be careful. Do not use the camera prop at a regular place like a bar or a club. The girls will think you are a total loser. At a fun, large event, a camera is more in keeping with the festive atmosphere. In a different setting, the camera will seem too weird.

Mardi Gras beads can be fun outside of New Orleans. Get as many beads as you can because girls love them and will take all you give them. These beads will guarantee making you the life of the party. Girls will be all over you for them, especially the necklaces with really big beads.

Everyone knows at least one person who knows about a thousand jokes. Telling a lot of jokes is all right for a group situation in which you have to talk to more than one girl at the same time. But eventually, it is time to go one-on-one with the girl in whom you are interested. Knowing a lot of jokes is not the substitute for a real rap, even though it is okay to have a few jokes in your head if you really need to tell some. The main problem with jokes is that most jokes that people know and remember are dirty jokes. Dirty jokes usually do not work well on someone you do not know. There is a big chance that a girl who does not know you will be offended if you tell a dirty joke. Your rap should stay clean unless it is obvious that the girl wants to talk dirty.

Some guys have a repertoire of magic tricks, brain-teasers or word puzzle games. ("Take these triangles and make them into a pyramid.") If used properly and quickly, these can work for a few minutes of your rap. It is usually better to slip these in during the beginning rather than at the middle or the end of the rap. Using them after the beginning may upset the flow of your rap. In general, these types of games are okay if you use them quickly and then move on to your regular rap.

Props and games must only be used in the correct setting. They are unnecessary at a wedding and impossible to use in a loud club or bar. They work best in a quiet setting where there are not a lot of distractions.

The main idea behind props and games is just to break the ice. It can be fun and cute if you do it quickly and then move on. Pretty soon the girl will want to hear your real rap after you have broken the ice with a cute prop or game. Thus, they cannot be relied upon automatically to give you a good rap. They can only make an already good rap a little better.

Picking the Right
Wingman/Run-Around Guy

Because most girls go out in twos, your "wingman" or "run-around guy" is a key and crucial element to your rap. (Also, most girls will think you are crazy if you go out alone.) As a general rule, unless you are going to a big party, do not go out with more than one other guy or wingman. Three or more guys hanging out at a bar or club make for a more intimidating presence to a girl. Many trendy bars and clubs will not let three guys in together unless they also have some girls in their group. Two guys on the loose laying rap make the best team. The reason for this is that two guys can hit on any number of girls together. For example, if there are four girls in a group, you and your wingman can talk to two of them while the other two girls can talk to each other. In comparison, four guys out together cannot hit on two girls.

In addition, as you probably know, working a room solo is very difficult. It can be difficult to find a girl all alone for you to lay rap on. Without a wingman you may appear strange to others, like the lone wolf. One guy talking to two girls is very difficult because the two girls may not figure out exactly which one of them you like. If they do figure it out, one girl will be reluctant to ditch her friend just to talk to you. And if her friend sticks around while you try to lay rap on your girl, she will get in the way and disrupt your rap. Thus, the extra girl must be dealt with properly and carefully by the wingman.

Everyone knows what a wingman must do. Your wingman must take the extra girl for you if there are two girls and you want to talk to one of them. The wingman must lay rap on your girl's friend as long as you rap with your girl. It does not matter that the girl's friend may be very ugly. The wingman must do his job at any cost. He must be able to pull his own weight and back you up. Otherwise, your girl may get pulled away by her friend whom your wingman has failed to entertain.

You must train your wingman often, discussing strategy and potential scenarios. During the night out, you should keep in close communication with him, telling him whom you like and how long you need him to occupy her friend. Like getting a good rap, becoming a good wingman can also take time and practice.

When approaching two girls, only one of you can initiate the contact with both of them. You and your friend must be careful not to step on each other's dialogue. Once the two of you get to know the girls a little bit (e.g., learning their names, where they are from, etc.), you and your wingman must each pair off with a girl.

Needless to say, you must often play the wingman yourself. If you are the wingman, you should keep an eye on your friend's rap. You should be prepared to help him if it looks like he is struggling. You must make him look good in front of his girl. Since he cannot necessarily brag about something he has done recently, you should be the one to introduce it into his conversation. After you have introduced the new topic, go back and continue your conversation with your girl while your friend continues his rap one-on-one. A good wingman will even run interference by talking to another guy if the girl you like is with some guy who is a just a friend, brother or cousin.

When you are the wingman, you should take the opportunity to try new things in your rap. It is a good time to fine-tune your delivery and attitude. Use your time as wingman to just practice the rap to keep it clicking and in good shape. A rap can lose its timing and technique if you don't keep practicing it when you get the chance. If you are lucky as the wingman, you may actually end up liking the girl you are talking to enough to date her.

When you are not the wingman, it may happen that the girl you like has a friend who does not like your wingman. This should not affect his role. He must keep talking to her and stall her as long as possible while you work your rap on her friend. If necessary, your wingman should tell his girl that it looks like her friend is getting along with you. That might prevent the other girl from distracting her friend away from you, at least for a little while. If the wingman thinks his girl might interrupt your rap, he should persuade her not to and suggest to her that she let her friend talk to you a little longer.

However, if the other girl is not a threat to your rap with her friend, the wingman does not necessarily have to keep talking to her. For example, if the other girl has other friends in the place she can talk to, or some other guy she wants to talk to, he can let her loose. As long as she doesn't blow your rap on her friend, he has done his job. The wingman need only secure the privacy of your rap and prevent, as much as possible, any interruptions or distractions by your girl's friends.

At some point in the rap, you must buy your girl a drink. The wingman must buy his girl a drink too. You should pay the wingman back for his girl's drink if he has "taken a grenade" (i.e., his girl is unavailable or unattractive). If his girl is cute, you do not need to reimburse him for his wingman expenses.

Try to have several wingmen on which you can rely on any given night. A friend of yours can hook up with a girlfriend and get married in the blink of an eye. You could get sick of a friend and not want to run around with him for a while. You need to have several wingmen at your disposal.

Don't waste time hanging out with poor wingmen. A bad one can destroy your rap, because often we are judged by the company we keep. In many situations, your rap is only as good as the wingman you are with. Indeed, a good wingman can make a huge improvement in your life. A bad one can ruin your life. If your wingman says inappropriate and crazy things, it can't help you. The girl to whom he was talking will tell your girl what your crazy wingman said to her. It will be more difficult to get a girl to go out with you if she thinks you are as big a loser as your wingman.

If your wingman is not doing a good job for you, tell him what he is doing wrong. It is in your interest to help him improve his rap as much as possible. Two guys with good raps are better than one guy with a good rap and one with a mediocre one. If a wingman keeps screwing up even after you have warned him several times, dump him. Do not go out with him anymore. If he asks you why you don't call him anymore and have been blowing him off, tell him why. After a few weeks, give him another chance. Maybe he will have gotten the message or will have improved his rap on his own. Blow him off for a few months if need be. Maybe by then he will be less angry with girls and have better confidence to help you.

As mentioned above, a good wingman must be willing to take the grenade. In the military, a soldier will fall on a live grenade to save the rest of his buddies. While his friend talks to the pretty girl, a good wingman must be ready, willing and able to take the grenade and talk to the married girl, the angry girl, the fat girl, the ugly girl, etc.

To be fair, you and your wingman should rotate taking the grenade. Often, deciding who will take the grenade will be a major sticking point during the night. You should keep track of who took the grenade last. But if one person's rap happens to be on fire that night, he should not be forced to take the grenade. That is only fair. A good rap should not be kept bottled up. A good friend should not let his friend take the grenade as long as his friend's rap is clicking well.

A good type of wingman is a guy who has a girlfriend or is dating a bunch of girls. That guy will be more relaxed and confident. A wingman that is married is also good sometimes, if he is not a stiff.

If you are the wingman and you get stuck talking to a girl with a boyfriend or who is married, then talk to her about her boyfriend/husband. Here are the easiest questions you should ask:

How did you guys meet?

Where did you go on your first date?

How long have you been together?

What's he doing tonight?

Where'd you go on your honeymoon?

Have you met his parents yet?

Have you been on vacation together yet?

What did you two do for Valentine's Day?

Asking these questions will usually get the girl talking nonstop. Girls love to talk about their great, fantastic boyfriend/husband (ugh!) and can't wait to tell anyone who will listen. The good news is that your wingman duty will now be easy and painless. You now just have to pretend to listen to her and be interested.

Often there will be only one girl and you and your wingman. As the "third wheel," your wingman cannot hang around and be involved with your rap with your girl for more than a few minutes at the beginning. As a wingman, he must be able to step aside and let you rap away. He cannot blow your rap by interrupting your flow and one-on-one scenario.

When the wingman is with you at the beginning of your rap, he must make sure that he makes you look good. He should never put you down in front of the girl. Rather, he will pump you up and make you look like a king in front of the girl, even while putting himself down if necessary. Eventually, he should step away and let you rap. He cannot pout if there is no girl for him to talk to. At the end of the rap, you can bring the wingman back in to spice up your endgame. At that point, he should further boost your image in front of the girl.

It is often devastating when your favorite wingman gets a girlfriend and can't run with you anymore. Be prepared. It will happen. It is only natural. It is why you are laying rap in the first place—to get telephone numbers, go on dates and get a girlfriend.

Try Not to Go Out with More Than One Other Guy

As mentioned previously in the wingman section, you should not go out with more than one other guy. The reason for this is that most girls go out in twos. Also, the most popular clubs/bars usually don't let in more than two guys together if they don't have any girls with them.

Dealing with two girls can sometimes get complicated. The friend of the girl you like must be included in part of the conversation. Let your wingman talk to the friend, but make sure you talk to her also. Her friend will definitely report back to your girl what she thinks about you. Girls are easily influenced by other girls' opinions, especially the opinions of the friends they are with on a night out. After a while you can start ignoring the friend and let your wingman take over so that the girls know for sure which one of them you are interested in.

A common problem occurs when the guy laying rap cannot pick between the two girls. He can talk to both girls, but at some point, he must pick one of the two. While talking to both girls at the same time, he must try to figure out which one has her switch on. He could talk to both girls at the same time in an attempt to figure out which one of them likes him. If he figures that out, he should focus his rap on her and, after a while, start to exclude the friend from the conversation. He must be careful, however, because in the end he may get neither of them. If he has not focused on creating a cohesive rap with at least one girl, he will come away empty for the night. If he did not choose between the two girls over the course of the evening, they may end up confused about which one of them he liked. Most likely, neither will go out with you if they have a dispute over you. You might like both of the girls, but you must pick one at some point.

If you do run around with more than one other wingman, your night will be more difficult. Girls sometimes do go out in threes, but twos are much more common.

If you go out with two other guys, one of you must be prepared to split off from your group if there are two available girls to talk to.

If you go out in a group of four guys, split up into two pairs. If you go out in a group of five guys (which is stupid), you must obviously also split up.

Be prepared for a weak night if you go out with too many guys.

Creating the best-case scenario for yourself may require you to be cruel. You may have to blow off a friend for the night if it means going out with too many other guys. It's done all the time. It's probably been done to you without your even knowing it.

The Trend

Sometimes you suddenly get in the groove for a long period of time. Everything you say makes the girls laugh. You are unstoppable, *bulletproof* and invincible. It will happen. It's okay to wear that lucky shirt five days in a row. Ride the wave as long as possible. Often it relates to the season you are in. You could have a good summer, a good winter or a good year. Tell everyone about it. It will reinforce your power and confidence. Reminisce with your friends about what you have experienced.

Word will spread about your master rap, and everyone will want to run around with you. People are always looking to improve their own raps. Coach new wingmen on what to do. Let them see you in action.

Don't worry if the wave stops rolling. It will happen, so be prepared for it. You may have heard the expressions "It's either feast or famine" and "It's either a rainstorm or a drought." You might go through a lull for a while. If the lull seems pronounced and is bumming you out, maybe try something a little different. Go to different types of parties, wear different clothes, switch wingmen and adjust the rap a little. Pretty soon the rap will be back.

To get your rap back, try to remember what it was like when you were totally bulletproof. That is the zone and mood you want to be in. Nothing should faze you. You should be prepared for anything and to say anything. Nothing should matter. Feel confident, relaxed and fun.

Do Not Dance

As a general rule, you should never dance. Dancing is a big waste of time. Avoid it at all costs. Most straight men can't dance without looking foolish while doing it. Dancing should not be part of your rap, nor can it be a substitute for a rap. Instead of wasting valuable time dancing, you should be using the limited time you have at a party to lay rap on girls.

However, some girls you are rapping with will demand that you dance with them. That is one of the only times you should dance: when you have no choice and the girl you are rapping with will get extremely offended if you don't dance with her. Dancing should really only be done when you are in the late stages of a rap and you are trying to close the deal, or when you think you will end up making out with the girl.

Don't dance just because some random girl comes up to you and asks you to dance. She is just using you. Her switch is probably off and she just wants to kill time. Girls often dance with any random guy just because they like to dance. If she really liked you, she would rap with you first and then dance with you later. If a girl asks you to dance right after meeting you, tell her no but that you might dance a little later. Turning her down will impress her and boost your confidence in taking control of the rap.

Dealing with Guys Who Blow Your Rap

Often you will be at a party, a bar or a club, talking to a girl, when suddenly another guy will interrupt your rap and start talking to her. This can be infuriating. Sometimes fights will break out over this. It can happen when you go to the bathroom or go to buy a drink for the girl or yourself. Sometimes it happens right when you are still talking to the girl.

Do not let it happen. Interrupt the guy in return and blow his rap. Tell him to wait while you talk to the girl. Be nice, but be firm too. Ask the girl whether she wants to talk to him or you. If she says that it doesn't matter, resume your conversation with the girl and pretend that the other guy does not exist. If the girl says she wants to talk to the other guy, then let her. In that case, there must be a reason that the other guy is in the picture. You can try to come back to her later on. But if the interrupter is just some random guy, there is no reason that you should let him blow your rap. If he interrupts your rap, do not leave. Instead, you should try to blow his rap.

If he lingers and won't leave you alone, you can introduce yourself to him. If he keeps lingering, tell the girl that you are almost finished with your conversation with her and ask the guy if he can give you a minute while you finish talking. Of course, you then take more than a minute to complete your rap and get the girl's phone number.

Act confident, as if getting interrupted in your rap is not something that ever happens to you. This will usually impress the girl and make the other guy embarrassed. He will often just back off at that point. Say to him, "What are you doing? You're interrupting our conversation."

Often, a battle may break out between you and various interrupters. Sometimes a party scene can get hectic with various confident guys trying to zero in on a few particular girls. You should view those nights as a fun challenge, not as a frustrating and irritating experience. It is you against the world as you stalk and grab your prey away from other suitors. Make sure you let the girl know that the other suitors do not concern you. They are just gnats or momentary distractions, unworthy of your attention.

Getting Your Expectations in Line

The most disappointing nights are those when we have high expectations for fun and it doesn't happen. It usually happens like this: A friend calls and tells you about a party that's going to be awesome. You go to the party and it sucks. At the party there are too many guys and very few girls (also known as a sausage fest, a cock party, a butcher shop, a hardware store, etc.).

Often we blame ourselves and our rap. But in truth, your rap didn't suck that night; your expectations were probably off the mark.

Don't ever get too excited about going out for the night. Expect to have fun, but know ahead of time that it's not guaranteed. New Year's Eve usually stinks compared to our expectations.

The best rule is: *If you don't feel like going out for the night, that is the night you should go out*. When you don't expect to have a good time, you almost always do. When you expect to have the greatest night of your life, you don't.

Before you go out for the night, it is important that you have some idea of what is in store for you. Are you going to a party at someone's house? A wedding? A bar? A charity/fund-raiser event? Each situation is different and requires a different strategy.

A Party at Someone's House/Apartment

Here people are on their best behavior and are less likely to be mean and insulting. It is sometimes hard to get more than one phone number at a small house party because you don't necessarily want one girl to see you hitting on other girls. If you want to hit on more than one girl at a small gathering, there is an easy trick to use. Do not ask any one girl for her phone number. Get enough information so that you can call her in the future. Just find out her first name, where she works and in what department. Don't tip the girl off that you intend to call her. Leave the rest of your rap the same. That way, if two girls on whom you laid rap talk to each other about you, neither can say that you asked her out or that you said you would call her.

You don't really need a girl's last name if you are going to call her at work in a specific department. A department will usually only have one Susan, one Amy or one Rachel.

Even if there is more than one, talking to the wrong one is not a big deal:

You: "Is this Amy from the party at Mike's house on Saturday?"

Answer: "No."

You: "Oh, then I have the wrong Amy.
What's the other Amy's extension?"

Not asking a girl's last name during your rap will make the girl less likely to think that you will be calling her. That way you will be able to lay rap on several girls at a party without any one girl thinking you will definitely call.

In the long run, the girls will like you more. One gripe many girls have about men is that they ask for their phone number and then never call them. They don't realize that asking for a phone number is often just a way of ending a conversation. The quickest and most cruel way of ending a rap on a girl you don't like is to ask for her phone number and then tell her you'll talk to her soon. Thus, not asking for a girl's phone number will make her pleasantly surprised when you track her down and call her at work.

But if the party is big enough, you should be able to talk to other girls without much problem. If the first girl sees you talking to other girls, it can only help you seem more desirable. Talking to girls who are just your friends will also make you seem more desirable to girls you are interested in. This situation is known as creating "a perceived demand." If a girl perceives a demand for you by other girls, she will automatically be interested in you. It is only human nature to want something that others want. In subtle ways, you should try to make girls you like believe that other girls are interested in you. Do not brag that all girls want to sleep with you. Do not tell a story about sleeping with a girl or about a one-night stand. Do not tell a story about how you were mean to a girl. Do not talk about ex-girlfriends. Just be cool and make it clear that no girl has ever dumped you and that you do not have a problem rapping with girls. Talking about bad first dates is always a good topic of conversation. It makes you look good by showing that you get dates. It also shows that you are not desperate because you are capable of rejecting girls you don't like. Creating a perceived demand for you by *some* girls will make *all* girls want to date you. As many guys know, when you have a girlfriend, more girls suddenly become interested in you.

If you are interested in more than one girl at a party, try not to make it too obvious that you are hitting on other girls. And if the first girl you rapped with has no problem flirting with other guys at the party, you should naturally go ahead and rap with other girls.

Even if you really like one girl you have already talked to, do not ever stare at her as she talks to other guys at the party. Leave her alone and ignore her as much as possible. You already have her phone number or know where to call her.

A Small Bar

A small bar is a lot like a small party, except that people aren't necessarily on their best behavior in a bar. You should try to stand in the most crowded area of any bar. Interactions between people are much more relaxed and smooth in a crowded area since people are constantly bumping into one another. When you bump into a girl you like, just say "Hi, how are you? What's your name?" In a less crowded area, it is more awkward to suddenly start laying rap on someone. Laying rap in a more open area can make you and the girl feel more self-conscious. But if you are in a crowded area, it feels completely natural to start talking to someone right next to you.

After you get the girl's number and if the bar is not very crowded, it is good to leave before she does. You don't want the girl to think you've got nothing going on and need to hang out at an empty place.

At a bar or club, you must act quickly and start a rap on some girls you want to talk to. Girls tend to leave a place quickly if they are not having a good time and no one is talking to them. They also tend to go to sleep earlier and do not stay out as late as guys do. In general, their natural female anatomy does not give them the stamina of an average guy who can push himself to stay out late. Also, all it takes is for one of the girls in a group to get in a bad mood to cause her and all her friends to go home. You must strike quickly in this setting since there can be many variables working against you.

Guys will often stay out late hoping that the night will get better. Usually, though, it gets worse. As the night gets later, more girls go home and the ratio of guys to girls gets worse. The only good part of the late-night scenario is that any girls who are out that late know how to have fun. Many of them will be drunk and very friendly.

A Wedding

A wedding is the situation in which single girls are at their horniest. Laying rap should be easy. People are truly on their best behavior.

It is important to prepare for a wedding ahead of time. Find out *before* the wedding which girls are single and don't have a boyfriend. Seek those girls out during the wedding. Watch out if someone wants to fix you up with someone in particular at the wedding. That girl might not be pretty. Don't concentrate on the fix-up unless the girl ends up being pretty. You can forget the normal rule about not dancing. At a wedding, you must dance with a girl you are interested in.

A Charity/Fund-raiser Event

Many single girls go to charity/fund-raiser events to meet guys, not because they want to give to charity. These parties should be your occasion to load up as many phone numbers as possible. If the party is big enough, one girl may not necessarily see you hitting on another girl. This will let you get as many phone numbers as possible, but don't rush through your rap with one girl just to get to another girl. If you are working the party aggressively, you might be able to get the phone numbers of as many as four different girls. But if you really are hitting it off with one girl and she won't let you leave her, you probably should hang around with her for the rest of the party.

However, one problem that sometimes comes up at these events is that the girls can be cliquish. They act like snobs and will only talk to people they know. There is nothing you can do if that is how they want to act. They are just insecure and need the exclusive company of their own group to prove how important they are. Those girls have their switches off, and you should ignore them. The only thing you can do in that situation is tease them and ask them directly if they are talking to anyone outside their group that night. By making a joke about it, you may encourage them to let their guard down and talk to a stranger.

At a charity/fund-raiser (and a wedding), a girl will get dressed up and look the best she possibly can. Her looks don't get any better than that. As long as you date the girl, remember that the best she could ever look is the way she looked at the wedding or the fund-raiser. If that's okay with you, then you're in good shape.

At a very big party (250+), you don't necessarily need to rely on a wingman for help in approaching one girl in a group of four girls. It is understood that at a big party people get separated from their group and can sometimes be alone. However, approaching two girls with the intent of talking to only one of them will still be very difficult without a wingman.

At a big party, a large group of girls will often arrive together. It is understood among them that they can split off from the group to talk to guys. It is not like a birthday party for a girl's friend, where it would be rude for the girl to peel away from the birthday celebration and start flirting with a guy.

Don't wait too long before you start laying rap at a party. Best time to start is 10:15–10:45. As a general rule, girls go home early. Girls will also leave a party or a bar if no one talks to them. They may be pretty, but they will still leave if they are not having fun. It is no fun for them if no guys are talking to them. Thus, do not wait too long before laying rap. Otherwise, the next thing you know, some other guy will be talking to a girl in whom you were interested and you will have lost your opportunity.

If the ratio between guys and girls starts getting bad, be aware of it. Your time for laying rap may be over. At a late point in the night, it is hard to start laying a whole new rap from beginning to end. Again, girls usually go home earlier than men. They get tired more easily and drunk quicker. It is always good to cut your losses if you realize the scene isn't happening anymore. You can always still hang out late with your friends if you understand the likely outcome.

If there are only a few hot girls at a party and they are constantly being monopolized because of the ratio in their favor, be careful. Girls at a party like that get an inflated sense of themselves. If you do talk to one, don't be surprised if she is high on herself.

Always get to a party early and get acclimated. It is not a big deal to be one of the first people there. The person who is throwing the party will like you more. You can check out the scene and pick out the girls you are interested in as they arrive.

A Dance Club

This is the most superficial of all nightspots. Looks matter here. The music is usually so loud that conversation is difficult. Looks, clothes and muscles make the big impact at a dance club. Forget about laying rap; just try to look good.

A Group Situation (e.g., Four Guys and Four Girls Out Together for the Night)

Going out in a group comprised of both guys and girls requires some advanced planning with the other guys. You should all understand ahead of time which guy is interested in which girl.

In this scenario, the guys are not necessarily friends with the girls. As a result, it is usually better to meet at someone's house or apartment before going out for the night, and have a "pre-party." There should be plenty of alcohol at the pre-party as people get to know one another.

The television should be on with low sound in the background and one of the guys should be surfing the channels. Topics for conversation will come from the television. The radio or the CD player can also be on at a louder volume.

Remember that often the pre-party is more fun than the regular party, wherever it ends up happening. The rest of the night can involve crowded, smoky rooms and music too loud to let you rap with your designated girl. Do not minimize the importance of the pre-party since that is where first impressions are formed and major bonding occurs. Your rap begins at the pre-party and will carry over into the rest of the night.

A Great Scenario—Guys Out for the Night with Girls Who Are Just Friends

One of the best scenarios for going out is when you and few other guys (one, two or three) go out with a few girls who are just friends with you and your guy friends. This group dynamic will give you an immense advantage.

First, you can try to lay rap on a girl in this group if it is not established that you two are just friends. Second, if there is no sexual attraction between you and any of the girls in the group, you can use the girl/guy group as your "home base" when you are at a location. From your home base, you move out and grab other girls you want to lay rap on. In between raps, you go back to your home base and talk to the girls there.

Hanging out with girls in your group will make other girls who do not know you think that you must be a great, nice guy that other girls find attractive, fun, interesting or funny. Talking to your friends who are girls will automatically make you look desirable to other girls. Girls you lay rap on will be impressed that you are sophisticated and mature enough to have female friends.

Thus, even though it may sometimes be a pain to have female friends, it is worthwhile. They are a great resource for meeting other girls who are those girls' friends. The key to having a female friend is not to let her know just how much of a "guy" you really are. Do not let her get to know any of your bad sides, and don't treat her as rough as you might treat a guy friend. Otherwise, she might not let you near her female friends even though she will still try to be your friend. For example, don't tell her some negative story about something you said or did to a girl on a date. She might think that you will tell others about your experiences with her female friends if you date one of them.

Do not think you are just using the female friend. She is your friend for the same reason you are her friend. She has the expectation that she will someday meet and date one of your male friends. Thus, you should try to cultivate a stable of female friends. Not only can they amuse you, but they can also help you in other ways. A female friend will (1) invite you to parties, (2) introduce you to her female friends, (3) let you use her as a home base when you go out at night with her and her female friends and (4) make you look desirable in front of girls you want to lay rap on (i.e., create a perceived demand for you).

Smiling

Make sure to smile early and often. It takes only twenty muscles to smile and eighty-six muscles to frown. Smiling is easy. Frowning and adopting a mean attitude is hard. Do the easy thing and relax and smile. Honey attracts bees.

Do Not Pose

Some guys think they have to stand around and adopt a pose to attract girls. They think they have to maintain a brooding, cool attitude for the girls to be attracted to them. Not true. Do not waste time trying to adopt a pose or an attitude.

Instead, you should be concentrating on refining your rap. You can stand around and look cool all you want, but if you don't have a good rap, your cool pose is a waste of time. While you are busy setting up an attitude and trying to act cool, other guys are laying rap on the girls you should be talking to. Your cool attitude will come across in your rap, not in your bogus posing.

Always Bring the Tools of the Trade

There are certain items that you must *always* bring with you on a night out:

- *sugarless gum or mints* (for good breath)

Always beware of bad breath and assume that you might have it. Make sure you have a supply of sugarless gum, Tic Tacs and/or Altoids with you. Swallow Breath-Asure or a similar product before you go out.

Fruity drinks and any drinks with orange or grapefruit juice as a mixer automatically cause bad breath. Avoid drinking a screwdriver (vodka/orange juice), a greyhound (vodka/grapefruit juice), or a madras (vodka/cranberry/orange juice). Repair your breath immediately if you do indulge in these drinks. In general, almost all alcohol causes a little bad breath.

- *pen and paper* (to write down the girl's phone number)

You don't want to be caught without a pen when you need one. You don't want to have to rely on others to write down a number. You won't be able to find a pen when you really need one. Also, it is disruptive to the rap if you start having to ask around for a pen to use.

It's also good to write down other information about the

girl besides her phone number, like her address, work place and her last name.

You must be careful not to get caught writing down a phone number on a piece of paper with other girls' phone numbers on it; it is best to get her business card and write her home phone number on the back.

A cellular phone can also be used to take a girl's number. It often works smoother and easier than a pen and paper because you just punch in the number she gives you, call it and then hang up so it is in your "call log" phone memory.

- *business cards* (to give to the girl)
- *Chap Stick*

No guy looks good with chapped lips. But don't apply it in front of the girl; no guy looks cool putting on Chap Stick.

- *cigarettes and a lighter*

Even if you do not smoke cigarettes regularly, you might want to smoke on a night out to give yourself an extra edge. If the girl wants to smoke, an option is to smoke with her. But do not smoke cigarettes unless the girl wants to first; the girl might not like guys who smoke.

If you start talking about smoking with a girl and she asks you how much you smoke, always play it down as much as possible and tell her that you only smoke a little at night when you're partying.

If you are not adept at smoking, do not try to fake it because a real smoker will know you're faking. If you do choose to smoke as part of your rap, get some practice so you can do it properly.

Remember some of the surgeon general's warnings: "Smoking Is Hazardous to Your Health" and "Cigarette Smoke Contains Carbon Monoxide." In addition, smoking gives you bad breath.

At a minimum, even if you choose not to smoke, you must always make use of your lighter as much as possible to light girls' cigarettes. If you see a girl reach for a cigarette, immediately get out your lighter and light it for her. Girls always like chivalry. A plastic or fancy metal lighter is better than ordinary plain matches since matches can get wet easily on a night out.

Analyze the Girl's Body Language and Signals

Before you talk to a girl, try to get a read on her body language. Try to pick up her signals.

A girl with her arms crossed and a sour face should be approached with caution. Crossed arms are always a red flag. Next time you are at a party or a club, look around at all the people. No one who is having fun will have his arms crossed. At a good party, there won't be too many people with crossed arms, although there are usually a few party poopers in a bad mood. Crossed arms indicate a protective posture telling others to keep their distance ("Stay away" or "Approach with caution"). Bored or angry people usually have their arms crossed.

A friendly girl usually has an open stance. Her body language is extroverted and she appears eager to welcome conversation. You know some of the signs that a girl likes you when she is talking to you: her head is tilted, her eyes are wide open, she is leaning forward slightly and her arms are also open.

Be attuned to friendly female body language. A girl who is sitting down with her legs tucked under her is sitting in a very friendly position. A girl who is sitting down with her legs crossed in front of her and her hands on her knees is also in a friendly pose. A girl who strokes her hair slowly while she talks to you is in a relaxed, flirtatious state of mind.

Also look out for shy girls because their body language can be deceptive. Even shy girls who may seem to have negative body language will show signs that they are interested in talking to guys. Usually, they will look around and then try to look away quickly to avoid being caught looking.

If a girl has negative body language but you still want to talk to her, you might as well give it a shot and try to lay rap on her. Sometimes there is nothing more fun and challenging than trying to use your rap to break down a girl with negative body language. Converting a girl's negative body language into a positive, open and friendly stance is

not that hard now that you have The Guide. It will just require you to work a little harder than usual.

If the girl has her arms crossed, point it out to her. Tell
her what it means to others and ask her if that's how she is
feeling. She will then probably laugh and change her
body language.

Sometimes a girl's negative body language is just a de-
ception because she doesn't want certain boys in her
vicinity to talk to her. The body language may not be directed at you. Also, many girls like to play games with
their body language until they have decided that they actually like a guy. As Jean de La Fontaine said, "It is a double pleasure to deceive the deceiver."

And be prepared if you can't convert her negative
body language and are unable to get her to talk to you.
Her switch might be off, but that shouldn't matter because
you were prepared ahead of time. You should be confident enough to move on if you determine after a little
while that the girl's switch is off. The whole point of The
Guide is to prepare you for the many times that you will
encounter girls with their switches off. Those girls should
not faze you anymore.

A person's mood can change a great deal during a
conversation. Body language will change too, since no
person can stand perfectly still for very long while speaking. A girl's body language can go from positive to negative and then back to positive in a short period of time
because her emotions can fluctuate a lot during a single

conversation. Girls tend to show their emotions more openly and express themselves through their body language. Practice following a girl's body language as you talk to her, feeling her emotional ups and downs.

If a girl likes you, she will touch your arm here and there as a conversational gesture. This is almost guaranteed. Touching during conversation is a reassuring gesture that is inborn in all girls and women. If she starts touching your arm a lot while she is talking to you, it means she really likes you (but maybe not enough to let you kiss her).

If you have gotten the girl into this "touching" mode and she is now fairly animated, you don't really need the rap so much. Let her guide the conversation if it looks like she wants to. Keep the rap as a backup just in case.

If her eyes start really focusing on your eyes and she touches her lips, or if her lips start changing texture by becoming moister or softer, those are inborn gestures of extreme interest. At that point, she is thinking about kissing you.

You don't have to worry too much about your own body language. Just don't slouch. Your body should be strong, relaxed and fluid. You will notice that your own positive body language will come naturally since you are the initiator and the one laying the rap.

Make sure your wingman is also keeping his body language positive and open. A wingman with negative body language can be a virus that can spread and destroy your rap. As a test, you will see that once one person in a group starts crossing his arms, others in the group will also do it. Pretty soon the whole group will have negative body language and the conversation will become forced, defensive and repressed. Train any wingman you go out with to maintain positive body language. He should not cross his arms on his chest. Likewise, when you are the wingman, you have to follow the same rules.

Learning other people's body language can take a little effort. If you get a chance, take some time to analyze the body language of people at a party, a restaurant, a bar or a club. Notice how their verbal communication matches their nonverbal communication. With enough practice you will be one step ahead of the game as you will be able to anticipate what people are feeling and what they want to hear.

3

Developing the Overall
Rap Strategy: Beginning,
Middle and End

Every rap must have three distinct sections: a beginning, a middle and an end. Each section is important and you should not rush into a new one until you finish the earlier one.

Beginning

The beginning section of your rap is when you break in on the girl with your positive attitude. The beginning can be tentative while you are feeling her out, but it should be loose and relaxed. You are not interviewing the girl. You are asking a few questions here and there, listening carefully to what she says and using her own statements as the starting point of your rap. You are telling short, quick stories that become topics of conversation. It is okay to talk about yourself as long as it relates to something she might be interested in. ("Oh yeah, the same thing happened to me when I went to Club Med.") Girls complain a lot that guys just talk about themselves. Be careful not to go on and on about yourself. Try to make the conversation more balanced. The optimum balance is 30 percent about you and 70 percent about her.

By the end of the beginning section, you should know if the girl has a boyfriend. (See section entitled "Big Rule: Find Out as Soon as Possible If the Girl Has a Boyfriend," on page 74.)

Middle

The middle section is where the two of you are in the comfortable stage. This is when you can start to flirt more with the girl. Compliments should come more often. Buy her a drink. (Girls like champagne the best. Buying beer instead of a mixed drink will make you seem a little cheap.) Tell the girl that she is pretty if she is getting very flirtatious with you. Here your stories can be longer and have more details.

Do not buy or get a drink for the girl during the beginning of the rap. Only do it during the middle section. You do not want to waste time getting a drink for a girl who may not be receptive to your rap. Wait a little bit before you get her a drink. Try to coordinate with your wingman so that you both get drinks together for the girls.

The length of the middle of the rap is always the most flexible of the three sections. Many factors come into play here. Sometimes you have to leave in a hurry with your friends. Sometimes she has to leave in a hurry. Other times it might be too late in the night to get involved in an extended middle section conversation. If you are at a big party and you want to get other phone numbers, you should shorten the middle section and go to the end game.

Pick up signals from the girl as to how long the middle section should be. If she is at a bar, club or restaurant with her friends and has to go back and talk to them, don't expect to keep the girl occupied for a long time. Do your business and let her return to her friends. Ask her directly, "Do you need to go back to your friends?" She will either say, "No, not really" or "Yeah, I haven't seen them in a long time and I have to hang out with them." If she has to go back to her friends, don't assume that she is rejecting you. In fact, if you cut off the conversation first to accommodate her, it will make you look very smooth. Just make sure you get her phone number.

The same is true if a girl is at a big party with a lot of friends that she needs to talk to. You can't monopolize the girl's time at the party. If you spend too much time on a long middle section, the girl might be unexpectedly pulled away to talk to a friend. You must be sure to condense the middle section of the rap once you realize what the girl's obligations are at a party.

As one girl told The Guide, "A lot of guys spend too much time going on and on and won't stop talking. Even if I like them, I can't necessarily let them monopolize my time the whole night at a party. I might have to talk to people I haven't seen in a while. The guy should realize that and close the deal by getting my phone number once he sees that I am receptive. There will be plenty of time to get to know each other more once we go on a date."

Indeed, you should realize that it does not take that much prodding for a girl to give a guy her phone number and go on one date with him. Nothing is ever as hard as we think it is. A girl will want to give a guy a chance since she is looking for a boyfriend as much as a guy is looking for a girlfriend. What does one lunch or dinner date hurt for a girl? She isn't paying and she's getting dating practice and experience for herself.

End Game—Getting the Phone Number

Once you have completed the middle section of your rap, it is time to strategize your end game. The end game is when you start telling the girl that you are going to call her in the future.

The end of your rap is when you start tying up loose ends of your conversation. Close the deal and get the phone number. Remember: You don't need to extend the middle and ending sections forever if your goal is just to get her phone number. But if you want to try to fool around with the girl, the end game won't stop with just getting her phone number.

There are many ways to get the phone number. If your middle section is long enough, you don't necessarily have to go through the formality of asking for it. You may have gotten enough information to know where to call her. If, for some reason, you can't specifically get the phone number, make sure you asked her first and last name and where she works. Get the exact spelling of everything. (As mentioned earlier, the last name is important but not absolutely necessary if you know in what department she works—the receptionist in her department will know her phone extension just by her first name.) Write down the information as soon as possible since it easy to forget spellings during the swirl of the night.

A cool way of getting the phone number is by giving her a pen to write it down. Another way is just to ask if she's listed in the phone book.

It is not always good to rely on others (like a friend of yours who knows the girl) to get a girl's number after you have laid the rap. It is almost always better not to get other people involved. Usually, you don't want the girl tipped off that you're going to call. Also, she will most likely not want other people gossiping about who is going to call her. Sometimes it becomes difficult to get the phone number through an intermediate person. The person in the middle might say, "Oh, I have to ask her first if I can give out her phone number." Or the person who knows the girl might be unreachable for a few days and you might lose the opportunity to call the girl. You should always get the girl's phone number yourself or get enough information about her to call her yourself.

Again, don't always trust a friend to get the number for you. He might like the girl himself or he might be mad at you for some reason unknown to you. The end game of the rap is specifically there for you to get the phone number yourself. It is not there for you to fizzle out and rely on someone else to get a girl's number.

Sometimes an end game will result in actually making plans to go out on a date on a specific day. Maybe you talked about a restaurant, museum, sporting event or movie during the rap that you both want to go to. You can always change your plans later if you want (e.g., if you can't get tickets) after you call the girl in the next few days. But it is usually good to give the girl a specific agenda for the next time she sees you.

4

How to Create a Comfortable Rap Persona

A lot of people think creating a good rap means reinventing your whole personality and pretending to be someone you are not. That is obviously wrong. You do not have to be an actor and pretend to be an astronaut. You don't have to adopt a whole new persona. Developing a good rap is a complex, fluid process that requires flexibility, a positive attitude and a little quick thinking.

First, make sure you appear to be a balanced person. Do not let the girl think you are too one-dimensional (e.g., Mr. Boring Financial Guy, Mr. Angry Lawyer Man). Let her know your job is only one part of you and that you do plenty of other things.

Yet, don't be overly eager to impress upon her how well rounded you are. It should come naturally. A one-dimensional person is always very obvious. As Jay Mc-

Inerney explained in one of his books, a stockbroker is always trying to impress a girl by how much he knows about art, and a downtown artist-type guy is always trying to impress a girl by how much he knows about stocks.

Don't steamroll the girl with all your accomplishments. Just let them flow out in bits and pieces. Tell the truth without bragging or trying to impress the girl.

The persona you finally adopt will vary on different nights out. It should be created only after you have figured out the girl and where she's coming from. If she's a jock, talk sports with her. If she's into fashion, talk fashion with her. To do this, you will have to learn about fashion from your female friends, your sister or some fashion magazines.

Adjust the rap and tailor it to the type of girl you are talking to. If the girl talks a little dirty, you should too. If the girl is shy, be nice. If the girl is highly intelligent and well educated, use a few big words here and there. (Don't go overboard with a lot of big words. Talk naturally, but every now and then throw in a cool word like *tenuous* or *demeanor*.)

Expect the unexpected, and don't be too surprised when it happens. Girls can say some wild stuff once you get them going and you are working the rap.

Don't force a subject you want to talk about unless it is genuinely interesting. Try to talk about her interests unless you have some intriguing stories to tell like skydiving, going backstage at a concert, visiting a movie set or witnessing a crime or a juicy fight at work.

It is much better to figure out where she is coming from before you commit to a persona. Stay flexible and then commit to one that she is looking for. But do not lie and try to fake it. That is impossible. You are tailoring your persona to things that you know about. You are leaving out the things the girl might not be interested in and accentuating what she wants to hear.

It is the same theory as when a person is applying for different types of jobs. A smart person will create multiple résumés and tailor each one to a specific job. Although the résumés may be similar, they will be different in many respects.

You will not be able to talk to certain girls no matter what you try. You can't be everything to everyone. Usually, the girls you can't communicate with are looking for a very specific guy. If the girl grew up in a town where all the guys look and act the same, she is looking for those guys. If she only likes guys in tank tops who wear lots of jewelry, you are not going to be able to rap with her if you are not her type.

Big Rule: Find Out as Soon as Possible If the Girl Has a Boyfriend

It is never too early to ask if a girl has a boyfriend. Never do it in the first few questions, but ask within the first four minutes for sure. This is one way to find out if the girl has her switch on or off. If she's at a singles party, she doesn't have a boyfriend and you don't have to ask her. Again, you don't want to be wasting time talking to a girl who has a boyfriend unless she has a cute friend hanging around. If the girl to whom you are talking has a boyfriend, tell her you want to meet her cute friend.

A girl usually will not lie about whether she has a boyfriend. Having a boyfriend is so important to a girl that it takes precedence over almost everything else and is not something for her lie about. If she does lie, she knows it could jinx her relationship with the boyfriend.

Don't be fooled by a girl who flirts with you and makes you think she likes you. She may still have a boyfriend and her switch might still be off. For many reasons, the girl can just be teasing or using you. She might be out with her friends and just wants to flirt a little bit for fun. Maybe she just wants to boost her ego a little and reinforce her belief that If she's ever single again she will have no problem hooking up. Perhaps she's bored and wants to kill a little time because her girlfriends are occupied talking to other people. Maybe she thinks it'll help her job or career if talking to you could help her in some way.

Get used to asking specifically, "Do you have a boyfriend?"

Alcohol Is Very, Very Important

Alcohol is an important part of your rap, no doubt about it. Very few guys have such a good rap that they don't need alcohol. Those guys are naturally smooth and talkative. But 99.9 percent of guys in the world will need the magic elixir of alcohol to lay a good rap.

On some days you will feel so relaxed, confident and natural that you won't need any alcohol to lay rap. But on most days, you will need alcohol to help you. Because we are often dealing with our own problems with school, work, family, etc., alcohol will help you remove any daytime worries you have and get you in the partying mood. Use the alcohol to focus your energy on the mission at hand: laying rap and having a good time.

Drinking the right amount of alcohol to maximize your rap is a careful science. You can't just get blotto and expect to lay a good rap. Your level of drunkenness will depend on several factors, including how much food is in your stomach, how much sleep you got the night before and how much adrenaline is pumping in your system. Less food in your stomach, less sleep and less adrenaline mean you will get more drunk. You must control your level of drunkenness by keeping these factors in mind.

Remember that it always takes at least ten to fifteen minutes after you consume a drink for the alcohol to take effect in your body. You must drink just the right amount of alcohol to be buzzed, but not drunk.

Girls do not like talking to a drunk. If the girl figures out that you are drunk, she will stop talking to you. She will not want to give her phone number out to some drunk guy. She will not want to go out on a date with that guy either. She will not want to tell her friends and family how she met you: "Oh, he was totally wasted at a party and I gave him my phone number."

Thus, the key is to make sure the girl does not think that you are drunk. You must stay in control of your buzz and give yourself a smooth, confident rap, not a drunken, stupid one. If you are drunk and the girl is as drunk as you are, you will have an even bigger advantage. Everyone knows alcohol gives you an inflated feeling of self-worth and self-confidence. And that's a good thing. Alcohol can be your best friend. Harness the power and get happy. But remember that too much of anything, even a good thing, can become a problem. That is your challenge: controlling your buzz— not just when you start your night, but throughout the night.

If you feel your legs getting rubbery, you have drunk enough alcohol. If you want to sober yourself up during the night, go to the bathroom often as soon as you feel the urge. Emptying the bladder will create more room in the bladder for your body to metabolize more alcohol. This will sober you up faster, but it is not a magic cure. You will still be somewhat drunk.

To further help you sober up, drink twice as much water as the amount of alcohol that you have already drunk. Alcohol has a chemical that causes your body to release much more water, vitamins, salt and other minerals than normal when you urinate. As a result, you must drink much more water than alcohol already consumed to get your body back to normal. Eating salty things like bar pretzels will also replace salt you've lost.

Throwing up after drinking happens when your body is unable to metabolize any more alcohol. If you drink way, way too much, your body will try to expel the alcohol by throwing it up before any more gets in your bloodstream. You wake up with a hangover headache because (1) you have upset the normal chemical balance in your body and (2) the chemical imbalance and the alcohol still in your bloodstream when you went to sleep has disturbed your brain's ability to enter REM sleep. REM sleep is when dreams occur and is necessary for you not to feel sleepy the next day. If you don't get three and a half hours of REM sleep out of approximately seven hours of total sleep, you will feel tired the next day.

Thus, a key part of drinking alcohol is knowing what your body can handle. You should know how long it takes you to metabolize certain amounts of alcohol. Do not follow what the other people around you are drinking. Each person is different. Everyone will have different amounts of food in their stomachs and different abilities to metabolize alcohol.

Your ability to metabolize alcohol will depend mainly on what shape your body is in. If you are in good aerobic condition, your heart will pump blood quicker and your tissues will break down the alcohol quicker. If you stop working out for a while, you will notice that your hangover will be worse.

If the Girl Walks Away During Your Rap

If a girl likes you, she won't walk away until she is sure you will call her for a date. Remember that having a boyfriend and/or getting married is more important to girls than you might think. Girls have a biological clock. They talk mostly about guys when they talk to each other, while guys talk about a lot of other subjects together.

A girl is not likely to walk away from a guy she has met at a party since she is trying to accomplish her constant, lifelong mission: finding a boyfriend (and/or future husband). Why should she walk away before ensuring that you will call her? Once that is in the bag, she might leave you to take care of other party obligations (e.g., saying hello to friends or helping a friend escape a guy she doesn't like).

If a girl really likes you, she might not leave you alone for more than a minute for the rest of the night. She may have to go to the bathroom or she may be interrupted by a friend that she has to talk to. But if she's really into you, she'll be back right away. If she excuses herself, expect her to say that she'll be right back. If she says, "It was nice meeting you," while you are still laying rap, she is ending the rap. Forget her. She has her switch off. Let her go talk to her boring friend.

If a girl walks away, let her and don't complain about it. You don't care. If she likes you, she'll be back. If you really like the girl and want to keep pursuing her, go ahead and give it a shot. But remember, the odds are against you so be prepared to fail. If you have the confidence described in The Guide, a rejection by this girl shouldn't matter. Your attempt to continue to lay rap on her should just be practice. Maybe you can "repair the damage" that caused her to walk away. Maybe there is no damage to repair because she has a boyfriend. Go ahead and find out.

Dealing with Other Guys

A minor area of laying a rap is knowing how to deal with other guys at a party, bar or club. Do not put down other guys in the area where you are standing. That is uncool. Guys will often do this to try to hurt the competition. But other guys are not your real competition. You are really competing with yourself to develop a master rap. Putting someone down or bad-mouthing someone creates an angry vibe that you should avoid. It makes you look insecure and petty.

Thus, don't put down any guys unless the girl does it first. Then you can join in the fun. You don't need to insult anyone unless they are truly drunken assholes and have knocked into you, spilling your drink, and haven't apologized.

Don't interrupt another guy's rap. If the girl likes him, there is nothing you can do. Remember, there are plenty of guys with good raps out there. (Some guys are just super rich, which helps.) Don't hate another guy because he has a good rap. You too can get a good rap with a little practice.

However, if it is obvious that the girl doesn't like him, a good trick is to get a friend to start talking to the guy while you start talking to the girl. Your friend runs interference on the guy while you start working on the object of your desire.

Don't Stop a Girl When She's Moving and Try to Start a Rap

As a general rule, do not try to stop a girl and try to start a rap while she is on the move. Many guys think it is good to start the rap on a girl who is moving because the girl is not talking to anyone else. But it is a mistake because the girl will not be ready for the rap. She will be too distracted to listen carefully to your rap. She is moving for a specific reason: she is going to the bathroom, she is looking for her friend, she is going to the bar for a drink, etc.

It is better to follow her as she moves (but not too closely) or just keep an eye on her. Start your rap on her once she stops moving and reaches her destination. At that time, she will be ready for your rap. If you jump in quickly enough, she will not have started a conversation with someone else.

Eye Contact Is Not That Crucial

One of the myths involving picking up girls is that eye contact is the most important factor. Getting positive and receptive eye contact with a girl before talking to her is always a good thing, but it is not crucial.

For many reasons, initiating eye contact may be difficult. The girl could be shy or she might be trying to play it cool and not show outward interest in you or any other guy. She could be standing at a bad angle where you can't achieve eye contact. A light could be shining in her face so that she can't see you.

Even though eye contact isn't necessarily that crucial, one good rule is that you shouldn't surprise the girl when you start your rap. Don't creep up behind her unexpectedly. Many girls are easily spooked and can get frightened if you surprise them and start talking to them out of the blue. The girl must see you coming. Get at least some eye contact, even if it's only for a second or two, so that the girl sees you approaching before you start your rap.

Even though you don't necessarily need eye contact to talk to a girl, if a girl gives you eye contact, you have received an automatic signal that she wants you to talk to her. A girl will not make the bold move of staring at a guy unless she is prepared to talk to him. Don't get nervous yourself when a girl checks you out. You should expect it to happen, especially nowadays as girls are becoming more aggressive than ever. It is obvious that, as time goes on, girls will be asking boys out for dates at a much higher rate than they do today.

Sometimes it is hard to tell when a girl is really giving you positive eye contact. She may look at you but it may not be the type of look that means "come and talk to me." You will not know for sure until you try talking to her. Sometimes you will be wrong and think you have received positive eye contact when in fact you haven't. Be prepared for it. Overall, however, you will usually sense correctly when a girl wants you to talk to her.

Initial Icebreakers: The Opening Line or the Pick-up Line

Much emphasis is placed on the opening line or the "pick-up line." Most guys worry much too much about using a great pick-up line. They worry: "What should I say first?" or "How do I break in and just start talking to her?"

One of Warren Beatty's opening lines is "Make a pass at me." Charlie Sheen has said, "I know you. We went to different high schools together." Nice lines, but they are not why celebrities get laid all the time. They get laid just for breathing on a girl. A good opening line is not that important and fades away fast.

The key is the *second* line. The opening line is quickly forgotten in the surprise of starting a conversation. The key is being able to follow up on the opening and continue a conversation. Move away quickly from the opening line topic and continue the rap. If you do that, it will not seem like you used any pick-up line. Instead, it will look like you just casually started talking.

The opening line should be a "throwaway" line, a casual statement. It doesn't necessarily have to be your best material. The great opening line that everyone talks about does not really exist. Your opening line can really be almost anything. Just mention something that is going on around you. If the girl's switch is on, it doesn't matter what you say first. Almost no one actually remembers opening lines, and they don't really matter. You just have to be prepared to follow up.

For an opening line, you can ask questions you already know the answer to. Even if you know the girl doesn't live in your friend's building, you can open by asking her if she does. Even if you've never met the girl, you can ask her if she was at a party where you think you saw her.

Asking a girl "Haven't I met you before?" is not as good as asking if she was at a specific party you went to. When she says she wasn't at that party, move right on and ask her what her name is. Now you are in your rap. The opening line didn't matter.

The truth is, you don't even need a real opening line. You can always say, "Hi, what's your name?" and then, "What are you drinking?" and then, "How did you end up here?" and then, "What did you do tonight?" and then, "Where are you from?" Suddenly, you are in your rap. Again, the opening line didn't matter.

If you really feel the need to use a brilliant opening line, say something about how you saw her across the room and were desperately trying to think of an opening line, but then gave up and decided just to start talking to her. That is known as the "anti-opening line" opening line.

Being flirtatious and forward with an opening line is risky. Trying something like "If you were a new hamburger at McDonald's, you would be McGorgeous" will work with some girls, but not with most. Telling a girl she is the most beautiful girl in the world as an opening line is more bizarre than useful as part of a rap. If you are really in the mood to try something like that, you should say nothing stronger than "Look at you, pretty girl. How are you?" with a smile on your face. When she says "Okay," then you say "Great. What's your name?" After she says her name, if you want to continue your flirtatious rap, you can say things like "I saw you across the room and I knew I wanted to talk to you" or "You should see the way the light is catching you. It makes you look very pretty." Starting off this way is risky since most girls are wary of extremely forward guys who might only be trying to have sex with them. That's why it is better to do it in a joking manner so they won't be as threatened.

Dirty opening lines will not work. Your conversation must already be leaning toward the dirty side before you start talking dirty outright. Again, when you do use funny opening lines, make sure the girl knows you are using them as a joke, not because you need to rely on them.

Get Used to Looking for the Wedding Ring on the Girl's Left Hand

Many girls complain that men are particularly clueless about realizing whether or not she is married. Every married girl has a story about a guy who talked to her for a half hour before he realized that she was married. You have to get used to looking at a girl's left hand before you talk to her. Get in the habit of asking yourself, Did I check first to see if this girl has a wedding or engagement ring? And when you see a ring on the fourth finger, ask right away, "Is that your wedding ring?" (or "Is that your engagement ring?").

Often getting a look at the left hand is difficult because you're at the wrong angle or because of the way the girl is holding her hands. But don't be lazy; make sure you get a look at that ring finger. And beware: Sometimes what looks like a wedding ring is not a wedding ring. It may just be a gift or a ring she always wears. And many girls (particularly European girls) wear wedding rings on their right hand. Thus, if you see a ring on either hand, ask straight out, "Are you married?" or "Is that your wedding ring?"

As many people know, there is nothing wrong with asking a girl if a ring on her hand is her wedding ring. She will be flattered either way. Also, it is a great way to open a rap if it turns out that her ring is not a wedding ring. Then she will explain where the ring came from and why she is wearing it. Example:

Guy: Is that your wedding ring?

Girl: No.

Guy: Oh, I thought it might be because it is on your ring finger.

Girl: No, I just like it. My grandmother gave it to me.

Guy: It'll definitely keep guys from talking to you because they'll think you are married.

Girl: Yeah, but that's good sometimes, like if I'm on an airplane and I want to sleep.

Guy: What's your name?

Girl: Sarah.

And so on. In general, remarking on any unusual jewelry that a girl is wearing is a good way to break the ice. Asking about a wedding ring is one of the best ways to break the ice because it shows you are clued in to what is really important to almost all girls: getting married. Men who can talk about weddings, marriage and relationships are instantly given higher credibility by women. Most girls view men as completely immature and unable to ever even say the M word. If you actually use the word *marry* or *marriage* in a sentence when you are laying rap, a girl will consciously (and subconsciously) register that you are serious boyfriend material.

You Will Not Get More Than One Chance to Lay Rap on a Girl

Do not think you will get multiple chances to talk to a girl in a social setting. As in other facets of life, first impressions matter. Girls are conditioned to give a guy only one opportunity to talk to them. They don't like it if a guy they've rejected keeps coming up to them repeatedly. They like closure and like to make a decision fairly quickly about whether they are interested in a guy. As one girl who gets hit on constantly said, "I give every guy a chance. I listen to his pitch and make a decision. But I can't keep giving every guy a third and fourth chance to talk to me. I'm looking to meet someone too, and I need to make myself available to as many men as possible at a party. If I'm not interested in someone, I have to move on."

Thus, you will most likely not be able to begin a rap, leave and then pick up where you left off. By the time you come back, the girl may have left, started talking to another guy or be deep in conversation with her girlfriends.

Accordingly, do not be lackadaisical when you start your rap. Don't expect to get another chance. From your own experience in talking to girls that *you* are not interested in, you know that switching gears from disinterest to interest is difficult.

But do not let this increase the nervousness or pressure you feel. Now that you know the ground rules, you should be prepared for the situation. This is why having a good rap from the beginning is important. In reality, you should think that *she* is the one who only has one chance to talk to *you*. If you have that mentality, then the girl will pick up on it very quickly. Confidence and inner strength cannot be hidden or ignored. If the girl thinks she only has one chance to talk to you, she won't leave you alone. As you know, there will always be another girl to lay rap on around the corner.

If your rap was interrupted or if the girl did not express interest during your initial attempt, you can certainly try again. However, your second attempt must be more creative than your first one. You should try another angle, but you can't be perceived as threatening or aggressive. Give her a completely different aspect of your personality than the one she already saw. If you were nice the first time, act tougher the second time, and vice versa. If you talked about work the first time, talk about books, art or television the second time.

Figure Out the Situation
As Soon As Possible

When encountering a few girls or a group of them, your first task is to figure out the story or the situation right away. Is it a birthday party, a group from work or a group looking to meet men? During your rap, find out as soon as possible how the girls all know each other. Are they recent friends, roommates or friends from high school? Which of the girls has a boyfriend or is married?

Be aware of the time. How long has the group of girls been out that night? Do they look tired, like they are going home soon, or did they just start the night out? Did they go to dinner first or meet at the event?

Examine the composition of the group. Which of the girls looks shy and which doesn't? Do they all look shy? Which is friendly and which looks unfriendly? Who is wearing a wedding ring and who isn't? How drunk are they?

Once you think you have a handle on the situation, you can make a strategy for your rap. Tell your wingmen about any initial information you get from the girls together with your own analysis of the situation. (E.g., "Two have serious boyfriends, one is very single and one just broke up with her boyfriend yesterday.") You should then decide who should talk to which girl and whether any guys should swap girls. For example, if it is discovered among the group that one guy and one girl are from the same hometown or are both rock climbers, they should talk to each other. You should try to match up conversations among people with an unusual common interest. (Everyone likes working out or going to the movies, so those don't count. We are talking about slightly more unusual interests like mountain biking or marathon running.)

If the girls have men in their group, talk to them as soon as possible. Are they just friends with the girls or are they interested in them? If the guys already present are interested and laying rap on them, your group should back off and wait until the girls choose to get rid of them. If the girls don't get rid of them, there is nothing you can do.

Sizing up the situation is also important if you are going in alone to talk to one girl. If a guy you don't know is laying rap, be patient. Interrupting his rap will hurt you more than it will help you. A girl may become interested in you once you talk to her but you have to let her make up her mind about the first guy on her own. A girl likes to make the decision about when to end conversations with men. As one girl who goes to a lot of fund-raisers to meet men said, "Many times I'll be talking to a guy and another guy will just interrupt and try to start talking to me. It's so shocking and a big turnoff. Can't he see that I'm talking to someone else? Can't he wait until I'm finished talking to the first guy?"

Sizing up the situation can sometimes be tricky. Be aware that the dynamic and mix of a group of girls can change in an instant. One minute the girls are talking only amongst themselves and making it difficult for guys to talk to them. The next minute the girls can be looking around to talk to men. What changed? Simple. The girls have finished catching up with each other and are now ready to talk to guys.

Similarly, the dynamic among a group of girls can change because one or more of them go home or leave the group. For example, if there is a very moralistic or uptight girl in the group, the others may act cautious or less fun. The uptight girl can subconsciously or deliberately exert peer pressure on the rest of the group not to drink alcohol or talk to any guys. Once the uptight girl goes home, the rest of the group loosens up.

Likewise, when sisters go out together, they usually protect each other and don't let each other get into too much trouble. Thus, usually the best you can do is get a telephone number from one of them, which is pretty good. Sometimes, however, one of the sisters goes home, leaving the other sister who stays out and becomes much more lively and fun. As one friend of the author described, "One time I was at a dance club in Las Vegas and my friend and I met five girls, three of which were sisters. One of the sisters was a gorgeous twenty-six-year-old newscaster from Memphis. She was totally into me but my stupid friend convinced me that, because her sisters were around, I was wasting my time. So we left them and roamed around for a while. Toward the end of the night I saw my girl again and everything had changed. Her two sisters had gone home, leaving my girl with her two friends. The three that had stayed were all now hooking up with three other guys. I didn't forgive my friend for a month."

chapter

5

Picking Up Girls in Public Places

Laying rap in a public setting (e.g., supermarket, restaurant, department store, health club, jury duty, street corner, train station platform, airplane or park) is also a definite option. Often you will hear stories about people meeting in a public place. It happens, but not that often. The reason it is not so common is that public locations are not specifically geared toward bringing single men and women together. Clearly, it is more likely you will meet single, available girls at a party, bar or club than in a department store where there are girls of all different ages and various dating statuses.

The most important thing to be prepared for in public places is that you will most likely have to lay rap in front of total strangers. Because you are in public, you will probably not be able to get the girl completely alone before you start your rap. There will almost certainly be someone nearby who can hear your conversation. But do not let that interfere with your rap or make you nervous. Do not change your rap in any way just because other people can hear some of it. Ignore those extra people and focus completely on the girl. In reality, those strangers won't be listening to you too carefully. They don't really care about you, and they are busy doing their own thing. In addition, your girl will be impressed that the strangers around you do not faze you.

Because you are meeting in public, she will probably be more wary than if you met at a social event like a wedding. You must make an extra effort to be charming and cool. You must put her at ease and show her that you are not deranged or crazy. Let her know as soon as possible exactly where you live and work. It is much easier to pull this off if you are dressed well and clean shaven. If you are not alone, that will also help to show the girl that you are normal. Once you get to the stage where you think you can get her telephone number, ask her out for lunch or drinks after work. Don't pressure her to go out on a very serious first date. Make the first date casual and quick. This will help reassure the girl who may be nervous about going on a date with a total stranger.

Whether a girl has her switch on or off will become very apparent when you hit on her in a public place. If a girl has her switch off, she will let you know very quickly. It is highly likely that she will be rude about it because there are none of society's influences preventing her from doing it. If she is not with her friends or in a setting in which she knows other people, she may not care how she handles rejecting you. She may not make an extra effort to be nice while blowing you off. As long as you are prepared for a rude blow-off, hitting on girls in public places can be a definite option.

A girl with her switch on will be receptive to a rap in a public place if the rap is done properly. Remember, girls want a boyfriend very badly. Meeting her boyfriend (or future husband) randomly in a public place makes for a great story she can tell her family and friends. "Oh, he was so sweet. We met on the checkout line at the bookstore."

Timing is everything when laying rap in public. In some situations you may only have a few seconds before the girl disappears or becomes unavailable. One second the seat next to her on the train is free, and the next second it is taken. One second you see her in your grocery aisle, and the next second she is out of the store. One minute she is riding the bus, and the next minute she has gotten off. You must move quickly and strike immediately. You cannot hesitate or you may lose your opportunity. For example, if you see a beautiful girl on a street corner, she is going somewhere and will not have time to chit-chat. Your initial line and conversation afterward must be direct and aggressive: "Wow, you are very pretty. Do you have a boyfriend? Can I talk to you while you walk? Where are you from?" Etc.

In comparison, if you are at a bookstore and she is

walking casually through the aisles, you don't have to be so aggressive and get her attention by commenting on her good looks. You will have more time to chit-chat and lay rap. But in both cases you will have to act quickly before you lose the opportunity to lay rap. On the street corner, the girl can be gone in an instant. In the bookstore, she may decide to leave the store at a moment's notice.

Reveal Information About Yourself As Soon As Possible

The key to picking up girls in public places is intelligently and subtly revealing as much information about yourself as you can, quickly. The main barrier to laying good rap in public is that girls (and most people) are very wary of strangers. You can't ask her any personal questions without also revealing information about yourself at the same time. Reveal personal information about yourself as quickly as possible in the rap.

Start the rap by choosing a topic that relates to her. If you are trying to pick up a girl on the street and she has shopping bags with her, talk about shopping and the stores where she has been. Immediately after that, mention something that relates to you. (e.g., "I went shopping there with my mother last week to buy something for my sister.") You have to make the girl feel comfortable and relaxed. You can't make it seem that you are picking her up.

She has to get the impression that you are just a happy, friendly and outgoing person. The way to do that is to mention things about yourself. For example, if you live or work in the area, let her know as soon as possible where and how long you have lived or worked there. Once the girl is relaxed, you can get personal information from her such as her name and where she is from.

Supermarket

If you see a cute girl in the supermarket, be careful about what you have in your cart. You cannot have too many purely "guy" foods in it. Don't load up on Ring Dings, beer and frozen sausage links and expect the girl to instantly respect you. Put some seven-grain bread, skim milk and vegetables in your cart before you make your move.

Asking questions about certain foods as an opening line is a standard technique. But try to ask a question that you really need answered to avoid making the question look like a blatant pick-up line. Unless you are an actor, acting is very hard. Avoid pretending to be interested in something when you really aren't. Ask a question about a certain food that you really want to know the answer to. Examples: "Do you know if peaches are better soft or hard?" "Do you know the difference between pink grapefruits and white grapefruits?" "Have you ever tried this cereal?" "Do you know if I should freeze this type of bread?"

Asking questions about fruit is easy because picking fruit to buy is particularly tricky (e.g., "Does this look ripe to you?"). Even if the girl doesn't know the answer to a question you ask her, it doesn't matter. Just keep talking to her. Say innocent things: "Is this your favorite supermarket?" "I saw you here last week. I think I cut you off with my cart." Eventually, ask her if she has a boyfriend. If her switch is on, you will know it soon enough.

Bookstore

As in the supermarket, don't hold a stereotypical "guy" book when you start laying rap. Don't hold any books about sports, war or picking up girls. If you have a book about picking up girls in your hands, use it as a joke or a prop. Say something like this: "Hey, can I test this book on how to pick up girls out on you? I want to see if it is worth the money."

It is good to hold a book with a female character in the title (e.g., *Angela's Ashes, Bridget Jones's Diary*) or a classic book (e.g., *Moby-Dick, Love in the Time of Cholera, One Hundred Years of Solitude*). Bookstores are places where girls feel fairly safe. If a guy is in a bookstore, he can't be so bad, right?

It is important to get some eye contact before you lay rap. Picking a book can be a very personal decision. A girl doesn't want to be surprised by a guy hitting on her while she is thinking about which book to buy. It will help if she sees you coming. Smile at the girl first and see if she has positive body language before you lay rap. Then talk about books right away and find out which ones she is interested in. What book is she reading now? What was the last book she read? Has she heard of any other good books? Any good books she knows to give as a present to your sister, your mother, your father, your boss, your niece, etc.? What is a good book for a vacation? Who are her favorite authors? Don't ask too many questions; ask just a few to get the conversation going.

Also tell her about your interest in books: whether you read a lot, whether you don't have time to read often, the best book you read recently, who your favorite authors are, etc. After the book conversation, you can move into other topics such as what neighborhood she lives in and where she works.

Airplane

If you are lucky enough to be seated next to a girl you are attracted to, do not talk to her right away. Wait at least an hour into the flight before you say a word. It will drive the girl crazy that you don't talk to her. You won't believe how interested she will be in you. It is only human nature; people want what rejects them. Talking right away to the girl next to you on a plane is too predictable and too boring. You have plenty of time to lay rap. You don't have to start right away. However, if the flight is short (i.e., less than an hour and a half), just wait a few minutes before laying rap.

If the two of you are getting along, your rap on the airplane is really more like a first date. Make sure you give yourself enough time to make your airplane rap long enough that you have plenty of opportunity to get to know each other.

Bus, Train or Train Station Platform

One of the easiest raps to start is with a girl you regularly see on your commute to work. If you see a girl you are interested in one day waiting for the train or bus, go back the next day at the same exact time to see if that is when she always goes to work. Once you see her at the same time every day for a few days and she sees you, you are ready to make your move. All you have to say is that you saw her on the bus, train, train platform or ticket line yesterday (or whenever). Don't wait too long before making your move and laying your first rap. Otherwise, she may become serious with another guy in the meantime.

To start, ask her the basics: where she works, where she lives, how she likes commuting. With this type of rap, you can become acquaintances first before you actually ask her out on a date. You have the option of spacing out the rap over a few days. But you don't want to use up all your best material in your initial rap before even going out on a date. You have to maintain a little mystery about yourself so that the girl feels she needs to go out on a date with you to really get to know you. Lay rap long enough to get a date with her and that's it. It will make the first date more exciting for her as she wonders whether this new guy she has met is "the one."

You will have to avoid seeing her in between the time you asked her for a date and the time of your first date with her. Otherwise, it will be awkward seeing each other before the first date. There is *nothing* you can say during that time that can help you. There is only a huge downside because talking more before the first date will (1) decrease the intrigue and excitement of the first formal date, (2) increase the chance that one of you will say something silly to sour the excitement of the first date and (3) make it seem like you two are more friends than potential lovers. Until the first date, you will have to leave for work a few minutes earlier or later to avoid seeing her. And if your first date or future relationship doesn't work out, the time you leave for work will change forever.

Jury Duty

Many people foolishly try to get out of jury duty. But jury duty is one of the best places to meet girls. Do not ever avoid jury duty. In this scenario, people wait most of the day and get bored. People feel trapped and need to talk to each other during jury duty. It is very easy to strike up a conversation with a girl during jury duty. Topics of conversation are unlimited and include the whole judicial system, how silly jury duty is, what type of case you want or don't want to be a juror for, and trials you, your friends or your family have been jurors for.

Restaurant

If you are lucky enough to be seated in a restaurant next to a table with a girl you are attracted to, take advantage of the opportunity. Girls love to eat out with their girlfriends, especially for brunch. And what are those girls talking about at brunch? Answer: boys or men. In a group of four girls at a restaurant table, odds are that one or two will be single. At a restaurant, it is very easy to break the ice and lay rap. All you need is a good wingman and a casual rap. Just make eye contact and say hi. Ask about the food they ordered. Ask how all the girls know each other. Introduce your wingman. (Use his name. Don't say "This is my wingman.") The wingman should talk to as many of her friends as possible while you lay rap.

If you are several tables away from a girl you want to talk to, you must use an aggressive rap. You can use the waiter or waitress (1) to find out if she is single, (2) to order drinks for her table and/or (3) to ask her to come by and talk to you when she is done eating. Alternatively, you can go over to her yourself with a wingman and ask her name and the other harmless questions mentioned in the previous paragraph. Unless the girls invite you to sit down with them, it will become awkward for you to stand there indefinitely while her table is eating. You should try to sit down with the girls if there is room at their table or you will have to leave. You can end the rap by asking for her number right there, or you can ask her to stop by your table once she is finished eating. You will need an extra chair or two at your table if you invite any girls to join you.

Health Club

A health club is not the easiest place to lay rap even though it might be the best place to stare at hot girls. The reason for this is that many girls are focused on getting in and out of the health club as quickly as possible. There are very few locations in the health club where a rap is even possible. Usually, there are people nearby who will overhear any conversation you have. Thus, you might try just being friendly to girls you are interested in over a period of time rather than asking anyone out right away. If you get positive feedback from a particular girl, then you should pull the trigger on that one. Otherwise, you should use the health club to build a network of male and female friends. Female friends are good because they have girlfriends you may want to meet and date. The waiting area for an aerobics or a spinning class is the best place for people to congregate and talk in a health club.

Before you talk to a particular girl, make sure she sees you several times over the course of a few weeks. Once you are familiar to her, it will be much easier to get her attention during your first rap. A good approach is just to smile and say hi to her a few times over the course of a few weeks while walking past her. Eventually, she will become curious as to why you haven't talked to her more. At some point you can ask her what her name is to start your rap. Like other raps you start in places where you might see the girl over and over before your first date, don't let her get to know you very well from conversations with her in the health club. Save the long and deeper conversations for when you go on a date with her.

Park

Girls are particularly afraid of talking to strangers in a park. But a great pick-up line in the park is, "I know you probably don't talk to strangers in the park, but do you ever make an exception?" If you run in a certain area of a park and see the same girl a few times, then you have the same situation as in a health club. Smile and say hi to her several times over the course of a few weeks before you talk to her.

It helps if both you and the girl are doing the same activity. If you are both roller-blading, it is easy to start talking by asking her how long she has bladed and where she likes to go in the area. Similarly, if both you and the girl are jogging, biking or playing tennis, you should start your rap by talking about your common interest. A rap in this setting is easiest if you have seen the girl in the park before.

As with all these public situations, if you get major eye contact and the girl smiles at you, then she is asking you to start talking to her. Don't be shy if a girl smiles at you or checks you out. If you are attracted to her, you should act on it and approach the girl as soon as possible. If you are not attracted to her, rap with her just for practice.

Coffee Shop

A coffee shop like Starbucks is another place that people go to as part of a regular routine. If you see a girl at the coffee shop every morning, make eye contact with her on those occasions before you talk to her. Talk about the coffee first and then introduce yourself. If the coffee shop is in your neighborhood, the easiest question is, "Do you live around here?" If the answer is no, then ask what brings her here. If she does live near the coffee shop, then ask how long she has lived in the area. Then start talking about yourself to make her feel more at ease.

If the coffee shop has tables and she is sitting at one of

them, position yourself to sit at a table that is facing her. Start the conversation by discussing something that she has with her like a portable computer ("Do you like your Mac?"), a college sweatshirt ("Did you go to Georgetown?") or a shopping bag ("Was Banana Republic crowded?"). If she is receptive and her switch is on, you will find out right away.

chapter

6

Questions and Lines
for Your Rap

This section has sample questions and dialogue for use in your rap. If you ever worry that you don't know what to talk about with a girl, this section will help you.

You must try to avoid making it an interview by just asking questions. That is an easy cop-out. Entertain her by telling her stories when you get the chance, and comment on her stories. The goal is to let her become comfortable talking to you, so do not interrupt her.

Questions you pose should lead into stories. Make the girl tell you stories about herself. You can then talk about the same subject. You can make something up if you think that is necessary, as long as you remember it later. Have some prepared stories about situations that happened to your friends that you can pretend happened to you. The more stories you have that relate to different topics, the better your rap will be.

Again, laying a good rap is not like conducting a good interview. It is about creating a conversation that includes questions, answers, anecdotes, funny jokes and personal opinions and feelings. You will have to do more than just ask one question after another.

As one gorgeous blonde told the author, "I hate the whole question-after-question interview thing. Going too quickly and asking me "Where did you grow up? What do you do? Where do you live?" can be exhausting. A couple of questions about me are okay, but then I like it when the guy goes off and tells a story. I learn more about the person that way and figure out if I might like him. Pretty soon, a natural conversation about some topic will happen."

It is okay to drop names of famous people you know or have met. But always tell her ahead of time that you are about to drop a famous name. It is funny if you ask her permission first: "Is it okay if I name-drop a little?"

Try not to ask a question in a simple, obvious way. Always rephrase the question to make the girl think and talk about herself. For example, instead of "What are you doing this weekend?" ask "Are you doing anything exciting this weekend?"

Throwaway Opening Lines

"Look at you, all dressed up from work."

"Look at you guys, on a girls' night out."

"Look at you, with your pretty party dress."

(If you are alone) "How long should you wait for someone if you're supposed to meet them at a party (bar, club, etc.) and they aren't there yet?"

"So whose birthday is it?"

"Can I have a cigarette?"

(Play around with the cigarette even if you don't smoke. Follow-up:) "How many cigarettes do you usually smoke at night?"

"I saw you before on the other side of the room. I noticed your outfit. What's your name?"

"That's a cool outfit. You look like (someone famous). And everyone tells you that, right?"

"You guys all work together?"

"I saw you at the bathroom. Always long lines for girls."

"That's a cool pattern (on your dress). Where'd you get that dress? Is it new?"

"Are you two sisters? Who's older?" (Always guess that the younger one is the older one because then they'll both be complimented.)

"Are you cold? You're shivering."

"Is that a (type of drink she is drinking)? Is it tasty? What do you usually drink when you go out?"

"Do you have a suntan? Where'd you get it?

"I'll buy you whatever drink you want because tonight is your night."

"Hi, how are you?"

The Job Questions

"Where do you work?"

This is the most boring of all questions. Do not ask it right away. You should be talking for a while about other things before you get to this question. Once you do ask it (or it is asked of you), you can make a game out of it and try to guess where she works (or make her guess where you work). The guessing game can be used for a lot of questions and is fun if done quickly and not drawn out. The key is to make your guesses funny.

The guessing game can also be used for questions like "Where are you from?" "How old are you?" "How many brothers and sisters do you have?" and "When's your birthday?"

Question: "What do you do?"

Answers: Bowling shoe disinfector, astronaut, understudy for (famous actor) in (famous play/musical) on Broadway, oil-well firefighter, illegal cable box dealer, etc.

As part of your rap, try not to start talking about work right away. This topic should come eventually and naturally. The best thing is to start talking about your work if you have a specific funny story that relates to it. Otherwise, it should come up only after she asks you about it. It always looks bad when a guy just starts talking out of the blue about where he works. You should not try to impress the girl in such an obvious way. But once she starts asking you about your work, it is all right to go into it more.

It is usually more interesting to talk about people at work rather than specific business deals you might be working on. In general, people are most interested in relationships (romantic, competitive, adversarial) rather than specific business-type transactions. Girls are especially interested in interpersonal relationships rather than professional issues.

Analyzing popular entertainment also shows us how you should tailor your rap. Sitcoms, currently the most popular type of television programs, are the best window into seeing what girls are interested in. The nonfamily-oriented sitcoms will spend most of the time dealing with interpersonal relationships. Although they may be set in an office or other work environment, they tend to be about the characters' relationships with one another. TV shows are all about who is sleeping with whom, who has a crush on whom, who is mad at whom, who is hiding something from whom, etc.

Just like sitcoms are giving the audience what they want, you should give the girl what she wants. Do not talk about the specific fine points of some business deal you are working on; instead, after describing the deal in general, try to talk about the people involved in the deal.

When talking about your job, do not say anything bad about it even if you hate it, unless it is a part-time or a summer job. In that case, it is all right to complain about it, as many funny and amusing stories come out of part-time jobs. Again, you must come across as being able to handle anything. By complaining about your job, you will seem weak. You can say that you have a tough boss or that you are looking to switch jobs, but do not say that you hate your job. No girl wants to go out with a guy who complains all the time about his job and who is unhappy every day he goes to work.

Instead, just talk about the positive parts of your job. Also, you can tell anecdotes about bad things that may have happened to you at work, but you cannot give the impression that you are unhappy there. You can talk about some minor, funny problems at work, but make it look like you are happy at work overall.

When the girl talks about her job, you must make a big deal about it. Act intently interested and compliment her about it. Just like having a boyfriend, many girls wrap their self-worth up in their stupid jobs. Guys know that jobs are no big deal and that they are all pretty much interchangeable. You will see, however, that many girls obsess about their jobs and are so into them that it is bizarre. But you will use that to your advantage. As smoothly as possible, without acting phony, go along with the girl and validate her internal feeling that her job is great and that what she does is important. You should not minimize her job like most guys do without thinking carefully. If you act interested and respectful of her job, she will think you are quite different from most guys who are more insensitive about how important her job is to her.

Talking about work during your rap can be tricky. There is no need to talk about it forever since it will eventually get boring. You must be able to move on quickly to other topics once the work talk is through. Many guys have no rap because work is pretty much all they have to talk about. You are not one of those guys.

You will notice that in many raps you lay, the work issue may never even come up. In reality, you must be aware that there are many, many things to talk about in a rap besides work. You could spend the whole night talking to a girl and work will never even be mentioned. Those are the best girls. On those nights that the work rap is not an issue, you will see that you most likely have laid a better rap than usual. You must understand that the work rap should only be a very small, minor part of your entire rap. Many guys think it is the most important part of a rap and spend a lot of wasteful time thinking about it. In reality, the work rap is not as important as most people think.

Other work-related questions include:

"Is your office near here?"

"Is your boss nice to you?"

"Any good office gossip?"

"Do people hook up in the office?"

"Has anyone ever gotten caught fooling around in the office?"

"Any wild Christmas party stories?"

"What are your favorite websites you surf at work?"

When a girl asks you where you work, it is often a code question. In her mind the answer to the question will reveal many things including how much money you make. This brings us to another rule: Never talk directly about money during your rap. Do not say that this thing or that item was expensive or a rip-off. Do not say that you are happy you got a good deal on something at the department store. Do not complain that some restaurant was too expensive or overpriced. Don't make her think you are cheap or frugal, even if you are.

Instead, your job is to make the girl think that money is not an issue with you. If something is too expensive, it should not be a big deal—you can handle it. Money should not be part of the rap at all. If she starts talking about money or how expensive something might be, do not play along and agree with her. Don't put her down, but make her understand that money is not a problem with you. Say you hadn't really thought about it and change the subject.

It is easy to impress the girl about money you have or about money that you spend without being direct and obvious about it. Just talk about future and past vacations. If you are talking about shopping, tell her how you bought the first thing you liked because you didn't feel like shopping around. She will think you bought the first thing because money is not an issue. Also, if you don't make an issue about money, she will think you have plenty of it.

Follow-up Questions

After you have been in your rap for a few minutes, you may hit a wall. Here are some questions you can ask to keep your rap moving:

"How do you guys know each other?" (when talking to girls in a group)

"Have you been to (new, trendy restaurant)?" (There is usually one new restaurant that everyone is talking about.)

"Where are you from?"

"What sports do you like?"

"Oh, you like basketball. Do you get a lot of marriage proposals right after you tell a guy that?"

"Who are you here with tonight?"

"What are your favorite websites?"

The Hygiene and Wardrobe Questions

One of the first things you should do is compliment the girl on what she is wearing. This is very important. A girl makes a huge effort deciding what she is going to wear at night. If you compliment her on it, you will automatically score major points very early.

"That's a great outfit. Did you wear that to work today? Where did you get it?"

"Is that a new hairstyle? It's beautiful. Much better than (name a famous actress with a popular haircut)."

"Where do you have your hair done? Do you go to (name of popular salon in your city)?"

"Can I feel your shirt? (Don't wait for an answer, touch the sleeve of her shirt.) Ooh, it's cotton. Where'd you get it?"

"Y'know, you only have a week (two weeks, one month, etc.) left to wear white before it's fall."

"Did you put lipstick on in the bathroom? (Notice if she put lipstick on and comment that you like the color.)

"I like your shoes. Is that a chunky heel? Is that a wedge heel?"

"That's cool nail polish. Are all your nails real? Did you do them today? Is that 'Hard Candy' or 'Urban Decay?'"

"What's your name?" (Flirtatious response after hearing her name:) "Oh, a pretty name for a pretty girl."

"Can I tell you something? You have great hair."

"You have very nice teeth, did you have braces when you were a child?"

(Smell her neck.) "Is that your perfume? It's nice. Is it (Dior, Paloma Picasso, Anaïs Anaïs, etc.)?"

Flirtatious Questions

"What kind of guys do you go out with? Artists, lawyers, doctors, financial types, actors?"

"How old was the oldest guy you have ever dated? How old were you at the time?"

"How old were you when you first had sex?"

"Have you ever kissed a girl?"

"Have you ever been in a threesome?"

"What's the longest you've ever gone without sex?"

"Have you ever dated someone younger than you?"

"Have you ever been to a strip club? On a date? On a first date? On a blind date?"

"You have a great (nice, hot) body. Make a muscle for me. (Touch her bicep.)

(If she has a belly shirt, poke her in the belly and say) "Nice belly."

"Are you a good kisser?"

"Is kissing important to you?"

"Have you ever tried kissing someone and couldn't do it because you weren't in sync?"

Don't leer at her breasts or say anything about them unless she says something first. Breasts are the only part of the body that is off limits even at the familiar stage. Breasts are a source of constant worry for girls. They think they are either too big or too small. Various people in her childhood may have teased her about them. If you comment about them, the girl will become paranoid and think that her breasts are the only reason you like her, even if it is true. Lucky for you, every other part of her body is fair game—legs, arms, neck, hair, teeth, hands.

Some girls will wear an outfit accentuating their breasts and calling attention to them. It will impress her if you can control yourself and not look at them when you talk to her.

NOTE: Anytime a girl says something bad about herself, tell her she is wrong (e.g., She: "My job is not interesting." You: "No, don't say that, it is interesting"). Or if she comments on how she does not like her clothes, tell her she is wrong and comment that they look great on her.

Personal History Questions

"Where'd you go to college?"

"Where'd you go to elementary school?" (ask as a joke)

"Where'd you go to summer camp?" (ask as a joke)

"Do you live around here?"

"Where do you live? Do you have any pets?"

"Do you guys live together?" (referring to her and her friend)

"Do you work out at_____gym?" (Guess where she works out depending on where she lives.)

"Do you have any brothers or sisters? Oh, so you are like (name a *Brady Bunch* girl: Cindy = youngest, Jan = middle, Marcia = oldest)?"

"Do you have any tattoos?"

"What sports do you play?"

Recent History Questions

"What did you do for New Year's Eve?"

"What New Year's resolutions did you make?"

"What did you do for Memorial Day/July 4th/Labor Day/Halloween, etc?"

"Did you go to your five-year, ten-year, fifteen-year, twenty-year high school reunion?"

"Did you go to your five-year, ten-year college reunion?"

"Where were you on 9/11/01?" (or when any recent major event occurred)

"What did you guys do tonight?" (Tell her what you did tonight.)

"Where did you guys eat tonight?" (Tell her what restaurants you have been to.)

"Are you doing anything exciting this weekend?"

The Age Question

"How old are you?"

This question is only for girls under thirty. Girls over thirty might get offended if you ask their age. Before she answers, tell her you want to guess. Always guess two years younger than she looks, then she will automatically feel complimented. After she thanks you for guessing so low, tell her she looks so young because she has great skin (even if she doesn't). Girls place much importance on their skin. A "good skin" compliment will go far.

Questions About TV

"What have you been watching lately?"

"Did you watch (popular chick TV show) last night?"

"What shows do you watch in syndication?"

"What are your favorite shows?"

Other Entertainment Questions

"What book are you reading now?"

"What movies have you seen recently?"

"What actors do you like?"

"Do you have a crush on any?"

"What plays have you seen recently?"

"Do you like this music (that is playing)? What kind of music do you listen to? What is the last CD you bought?"

"Have you been to any concerts lately?"

Personal Questions

"When is your birthday?"

"What's your (astrological) sign?"

"Have you ever dated someone with your sign? How did it go?"

"Have you ever dated someone born on your birthday?"

"Can I see your dance moves?"

Questions About Her Vacations

"Do you get a lot of vacation time?"

"Where have you been on vacation lately?"

"Where do you want to go on your next vacation?"

"What places do you still want to see?"

Pick-up Lines

Although The Guide does not recommend pick-up lines, people always want to have some in mind just in case. Girls particularly dislike pick-up lines relating to their looks because they sometimes make girls feel too much like sex objects. Many of the ones listed on the following pages have been around forever. A clever one is hard to come by. The only time you should really use a pick-up line is as a joke. It is sometimes funny to use one after you have already started your rap. For example, you can ask her if any of these fifty pick-up lines would work on her:

Question-and-Answer Pick-up Lines

Guy: Did you hear the one about the pretty girl who said no?
Girl: No.
Guy: Now you have.

Guy: Did it hurt?
Girl: Did what hurt?
Guy: Did it hurt when you fell from heaven?

Guy: Hey, you know I've seen you before. Do you know where?
Girl: Where?
Guy: In my dreams.

Guy: Are your legs tired?
Girl: No. Why?
Guy: Because you've been running through my mind all day/night.

Guy: Did you hear that they are changing the alphabet?
Girl: No.
Guy: Yeah, they are putting U and I together.

Guy: You know what would look good on you?
Girl: What?
Guy: Me.

Guy: You know, you left something back at the bar.
Girl: What?
Guy: Me.

Guy: Can I buy you a drink?
Girl: Okay.
Guy: No, I'm talking about a Bloody Mary in the morning.

Guy: Did you thank God today?
Girl: For what?
Guy: For your eyes/body/legs.

Individual Pick-up Lines

"You look a little down. You could use a good pick-me-up. Get it? I'm picking you up."

"Can I buy you a drink? Because the more you drink, the better I look."

"I lost my phone number. Can I have yours?"

(You stop girl on the street.) "Excuse me, can you tell me how to get to . . . (long pause) where you're going?"

"Listen, I know only one way to break the ice with you." (Take ice out of glass and throw it on the floor.)

"How do you like your eggs in the morning?"

"Do you want a short engagement or a long engagement?"

"Do you believe in love at first sight or should I walk by again?"

"Is there an airport nearby or is that my heart taking off?"

"Kiss me if I'm wrong, but don't I know you?"

"The only thing your eyes haven't told me is your name."

"Can you talk as good as you look?"

"Can I check the label on your shirt? (Check label.) Just what I thought. 'Made in heaven.' "

"That outfit looks good on you, but it would look better on my floor."

"I'm having trouble playing pool. I keep seeing your face on the pool table."

"Is that a keg in your butt? Because I'd like to tap it."

"My friends left and I'm alone. Can I hang out with you?"

"If I flip this quarter, what are the chances I get some tail?"

"Your lips are wrinkled. Do you mind if I press them?"

"Your father must have been a thief because he stole the stars from the sky and put them in your eyes."

"Are you ready to leave with me now?"

"If I follow you home, will you keep me?"

"Are those mirrors in your pants? Because I can see myself in them."

"Do you feel magnetic? Because I'm drawn to you."

"Live around here often?"

"How do you like your eggs? Fertilized?"

"If your left arm is Thanksgiving and your right arm is Christmas, can I visit somewhere between the holidays?"

"I wish you were a door so I could bang you all day long."

"Don't stand in the frozen food section. You're so hot you'll melt everything."

"Are you Italian/Irish/Jewish/Russian/etc.? Do you want some?"

"You must drink a lot of milk because it does your body good."

"Excuse me, can you help me? (Looking for something.) I seem to have lost my congressional medal of honor."

"Haven't we never met before?"

"Do you mind if I use my cell phone? I have to call my mother to tell her I've met the girl of my dreams."

"Is it hot in here or is it just you?"

"Wouldn't we look cute on a wedding cake?"

"You know, if you were a laser, you'd be set on stunning."

"Can I buy you a drink or do you just want the money?"

7

The Postgame Report— Final Thoughts

After your night out, analyze your rap and how it worked. Think about what you could have done differently if you could do it over again. Did you drink too much or too little? Did you hide your drunkenness well? Did you give off a fun vibe? Think about what you did right, and remember to do it again. Think about what you might have done wrong, but don't beat yourself up if you think you messed up in some way. There will always be missed opportunities: girls you wish you had talked to, things you wish you had or hadn't said. Think of all the girls you did actually talk to. Think of all the positive, good things you actually said.

You will sometimes think that there are two types of raps: the one with the dialogue you actually used and the one with dialogue you wish you had used. Don't make yourself crazy over it. Laying a good rap takes practice. Although people say a movie actor is only as good as his last movie, you are not only as good as your last rap. You will have an off or bad night. You will go to a lame party. Be prepared for the bad nights because they happen to everyone.

"Mind-viewing" is a common technique in sports psychology. Athletes are taught to envision the perfect tennis stroke, baseball swing, pole vault or rowing stroke before they perform the act. Mind-view the perfect rap. Think beginning, middle and end.

Eventually, you won't have to think about how your rap works because it will come naturally. However, a little work is still always required. Stay up on current events, fashion, museums, music, movies, television, restaurants, plays, etc. Working your rap and improving it will make your nights a lot more challenging and fun.

Even if you don't educate yourself about everything in the world, The Guide will still give you enough material to have a decent rap. Practice and a good wingman will give you an even better one. The more topics you know about, the better your rap will be. If you're knowledgeable about a lot of topics, you will have many more options in how you adapt your rap and persona to the girl.

You do not have to read this book ten times before you go out. Get the basics down and do your best. Don't worry if you don't have The Guide entirely memorized. Even using only a small portion of the information in this book will give you an advantage over the rest of the pack.

As you know, most guys have no rap. Baseball players get into the Hall of Fame batting only .300 lifetime. Although your rap might seem weak to you, it will seem like a good one to girls who are used to dealing with hundreds of horrible raps night after night.

When to Call the Girl After
You Get Her Phone Number

The final part of The Guide is knowing when to call the girl for a date after you get her phone number. Again, this is an area in which a lot of stupid myths have developed. "Wait three days," "Wait four days" or "Wait until Tuesday if you met on Saturday." It doesn't matter. The truth is that if a girl likes you, *it doesn't matter when you call*. You could call her a month later and it won't matter. Just don't call the same night you meet the girl. If you met the girl on Friday or Saturday night, wait at least two days, until Sunday *night* or Monday. Calling on Sunday during the day is too soon. If you get the number during the week (Monday to Thursday), it is okay to call the next day or the day after that.

Do not wait too long, but the bottom line is that if the girl likes you, it doesn't matter when you call her. Girls remember every guy they meet, and they certainly remember every guy to whom they gave their phone number. Every time a girl meets a guy, she is analyzing him and deciding if he is boyfriend material. If she liked you at all when you met, even just a little bit, she will remember you and go on a date with you.

The best excuses for why you waited so long to call are that you were breaking up with your girlfriend and weren't ready to go on more dates or that you were traveling for work.

As mentioned earlier, an end game will sometimes result in having a date already set up for a specific day. Usually, though, you will just get the number and she won't know when the new, mysterious guy is going to call.

If you call her and get her answering machine, *do not leave a message.* But beware of Caller ID, which can display your name and phone number. Always press *67 (a free service) on your phone before you dial the girl's phone number. This will block her Caller ID and she won't know that it was you who didn't leave a message. Also, you can call the phone company and get your phone number blocked on all outgoing phone calls. In that case, you won't ever need to press *67 because a Caller ID box will never recognize your number.

Leaving a message on her answering machine will not help you in any way, so don't do it. At best, she will call you back at some random time and you may not be prepared to talk to her (e.g., you are coming out of the shower, eating dinner, watching the last two minutes of a basketball game, etc.).

If you miss her at home a few times, then try her at work. However, for a personal phone call, it is better to reach the girl at home. Usually, a girl is more relaxed talking to a guy at home rather than at her office.

If she is too busy to talk at work when you call her, find out when and where you should call her back. Beware: Nowadays, there is Caller ID at the workplace. Make sure you use *67 even when you call her at work.

If she sounds a little cold to you when you call her at work, don't worry. It is sometimes hard for a girl to talk to a guy in that environment. There may be people all around her listening to her phone call. She could share an office with other people or work in an open area with people all around her. She probably won't want other people knowing all about her dating life.

If, after a few days, you keep getting her answering machine when you call her at home and her voice mail when you call her at work, then it is okay to leave a message on her home answering machine. If you couldn't get through to her at home, it may be because she screens all her phone calls. In that case, you have no choice but to leave a message. Remember, if the girl likes you enough to go on a date with you, she will call you back. Guaranteed. A girl will not let a guy who could be her future boyfriend (or husband) get away. She will call you back.

If she has a roommate who picks up the phone, you have no choice but to leave a message with the roommate.

If you are "on the fence" with her (i.e., she is not yet sure how she feels about you), you can be more persistent and call her back if she doesn't return your message after a few days.

The key to the first phone call is setting up the right day of the week for the first date. Your mind should now be focused on scheduling the exact sequence of your next few dates with the girl. Since a girl usually won't fool around with a guy on the first date, it is a waste to schedule a first date on a Friday or Saturday night. You don't want to be disappointed when the girl won't fool around with you.

Calling very early in the week should allow you to schedule a first date during the week as opposed to the weekend. Scheduling a first date during the day on Saturday or Sunday is also good.

When you call to arrange the first date, do not ask her what she wants to do. You must pick the activity, even if it is just going out to dinner. You must have a plan for your date before you call her. You can discuss the plan with her to make sure she has no problem with it. For example, if she just went to the restaurant you had in mind, you should pick another one. If she just went to the baseball stadium for a game, think of something else to do.

You must pick her up. Do not pick a restaurant right near you and make her travel far to meet you there. She will figure out that you picked a place right near you and get offended. You must pick her up and drop her at home at the end of the night.

You should then try to get the second or third date to be on a weekend night. For example, if your first date is on Sunday, Monday or Tuesday, you could ask her out at the end of the first date for a weekend night second date. All girls know that a second date on a weekend night is an "action" date. You both know that at least kissing is expected at some point during the night, usually at the end of the night.

Sometimes, though, if you laid a very long rap on the first night you met the girl and you are confident she likes you, you could try for a first date on a weekend night. In that case, you are betting that the girl might be ready to fool around with you on the first date. If you actually made out with the girl the first night you met her, you have most likely advanced past the "first date" stage.

Using The Guide in These Cyber Times

Meeting someone on the Internet has become a completely accepted method of getting a first date. The principles in The Guide also apply to your "cyber rap." What a girl wants in a boyfriend will not change whether it is determined over the computer or face-to-face.

Before actually meeting the girl, your e-mails to her must be carefully planned and thought out. Following her personality profile, which lists her interests, you must write her exactly what she wants to hear. In your writings, you can create the exact man she is looking for. If necessary, take your time between e-mails to research her topics of interest to inform her of new things. Like in a face-to-face rap, do not act desperate by writing back right way after receiving an e-mail from her.

Never see a girl face-to-face that you met over the Internet without first talking to her over the phone. You should also get a full-length picture of her. It will be easier to talk to her for the first time over the phone if you have an image of her. During your phone call with her, you should follow The Guide. The phone call will conclusively determine whether you will want to go out on a date with her and whether she will want to go out with you. Act confident and fun. Make the girl feel secure and at ease. Your rap will not be that much different than your face-to-face rap. It should have a beginning, middle and end. You should be completely prepared for it and have it completely scripted out ahead of time.

Gabe Fischbarg is a practicing attorney and independent film and television producer who is currently producer/legal advisor to *The People's Court* television show. This is his first book. He lives in New York City.